Left Hand Cursive

How To Write Artistically With Your Left hand

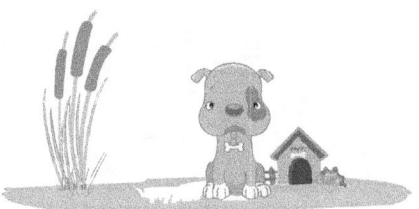

ISBN: 979-8-69-958459-8   Copyright © 2020 Derek Schuger

Introduction

This cursive font is designed for writing left-handed. It's neat, legible, and artistically formed. Here are the glyphs.

A	B	C	D	E	F	G	H	I	J	K	L	M
N	O	P	Q	R	S	T	U	V	W	X	Y	Z
a	b	c	d	e	f	g	h	i	j	k	l	m
n	o	p	q	r	s	t	u	v	w	x	y	z
1	2	3	4	5	6	7	8	9	0	;	:	?
"	"	'	'	!	#	$	&	(	)	.	,	

A quick brown fox jumps over the lazy dog.

To write this font, you'll circle the penpoint in a counterclockwise motion when writing toward the right; a fine-motor motion fit left-handed writing ergonomically. Writing this font is fun. It's all about rhythms of drawing counterclockwise circles. Here is the moving diagram of your penpoint looks.

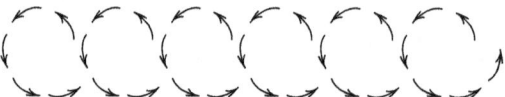

To better understand the concept, please trace the following dotted circles as arrows indicate.

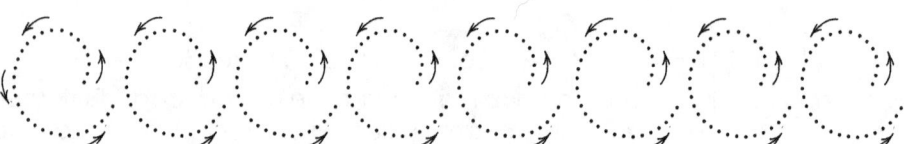

About Left Handwriting Posture

There is no absolute correct posture to write or draw. We see some people with awkward postures who write beautifully. However, ergonomic studies have shown that the posture below is advanced in comparison to others to write faster and easier. This posture avoids smudging and lets a writer move the pen or pencil naturally on the paper.

By the way, you may need to stiff your wrist a little and use some arm muscles to get smoother strokes before you master your fine motor skills.

Holding a pen:

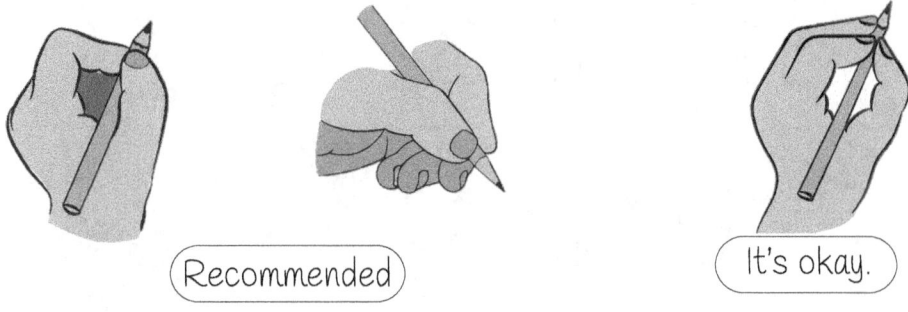

Recommended

It's okay.

Hand posture and paper location:

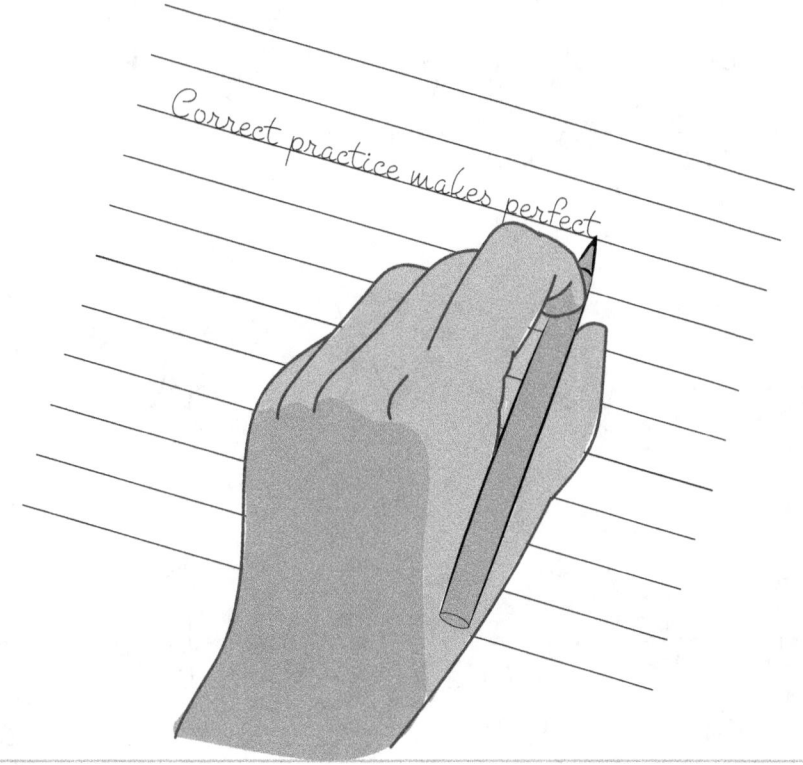

Correct practice makes perfect

Stroke order and direction are essential to keep the penoint moving naturally and smoothly, and they're clearly labeled for each letter in this book. Please trace the following dotted letters, as indicated by digits and arrow. You will have a taste of how to perform the writing of this beautiful font.

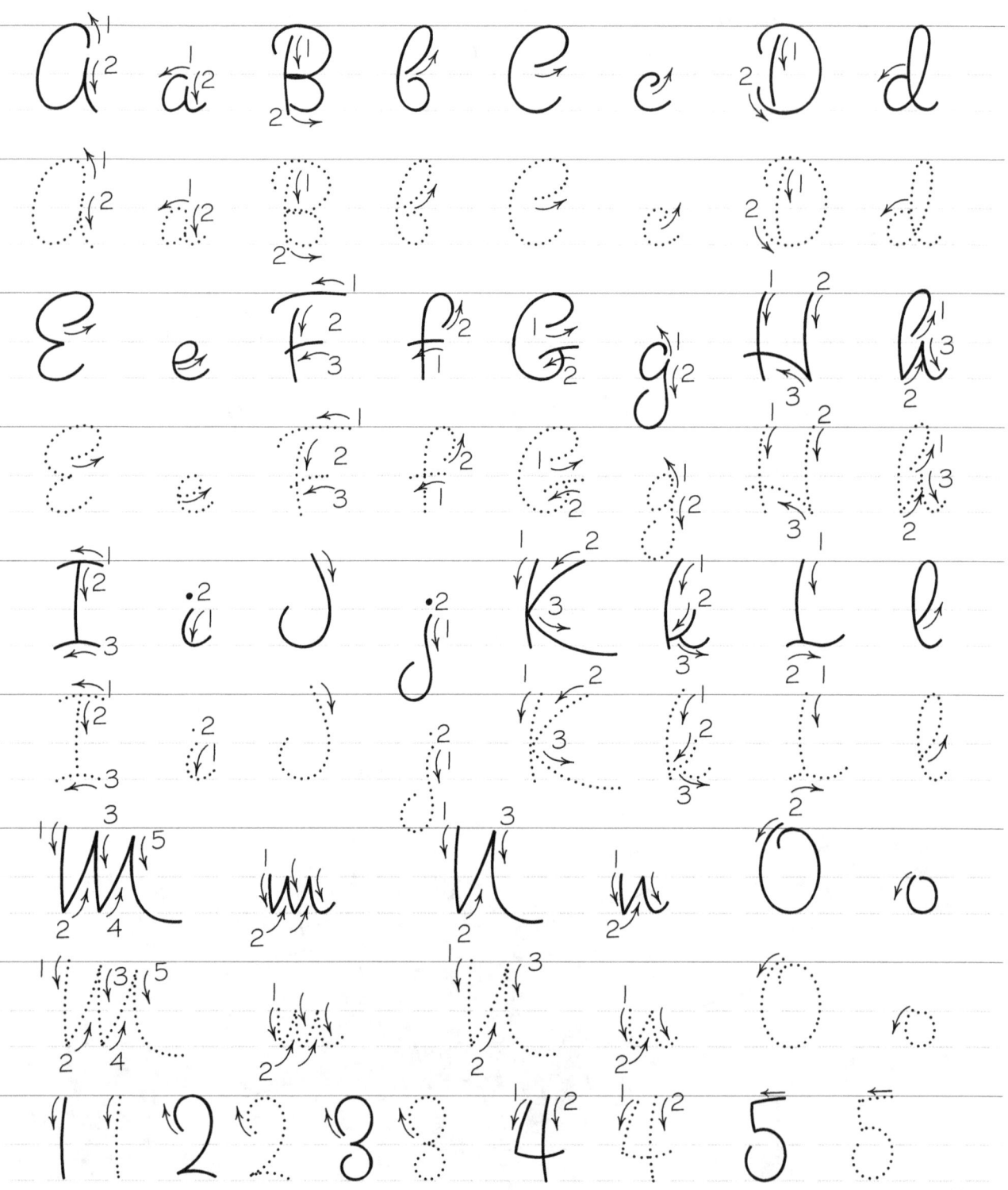

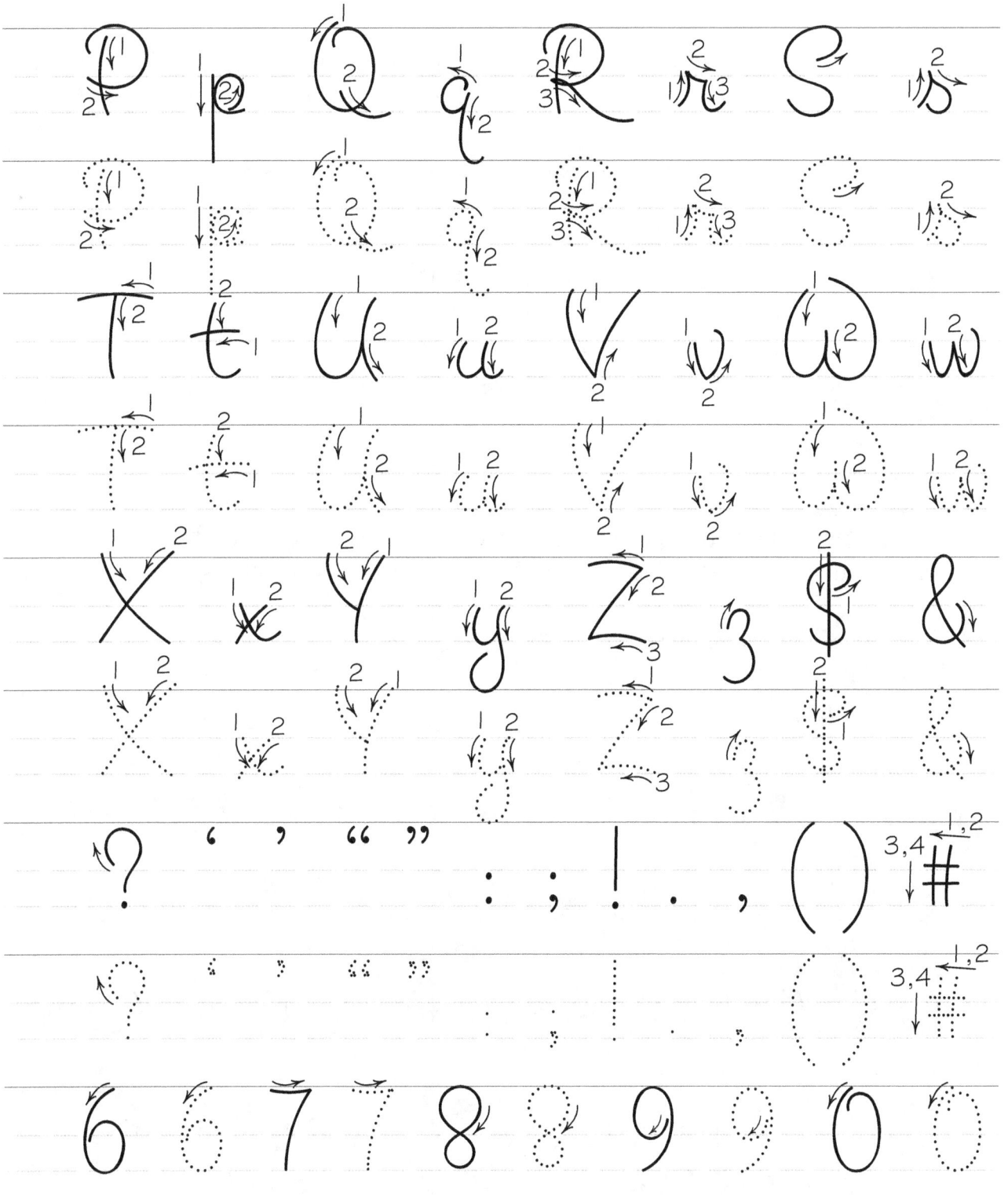

Pangram – all 26 letters of the alphabet

A pangram or holoalphabetic sentence is a unique sentence that includes every letter of a given alphabet at least once. Pangrams are particularly useful in typeface display, handwriting practice, and calligraphy. The best-known English pangram is "A quick brown fox jumps over the lazy dog." This sentence contains 33 letters with most letters used only once, except H, R, T, and U twice, E three times, and O four times. Some pangrams may not make much sense, such as "Pack my box with five dozen liquor jugs." (32 letters), "How vexingly quick daft zebras jump!" (30 letters), and "Jived fox nymph grabs quick waltz." (28 letters). But they are best to be used as sentences to practice handwriting or learn calligraphy.

The next page is some pangrams I composed, containing all the alphabet letters.

To master this font perfectly, you'll need to find a rhythm within the fine-motor motion of your hand. Please trace the dotted curves counterclockwise.

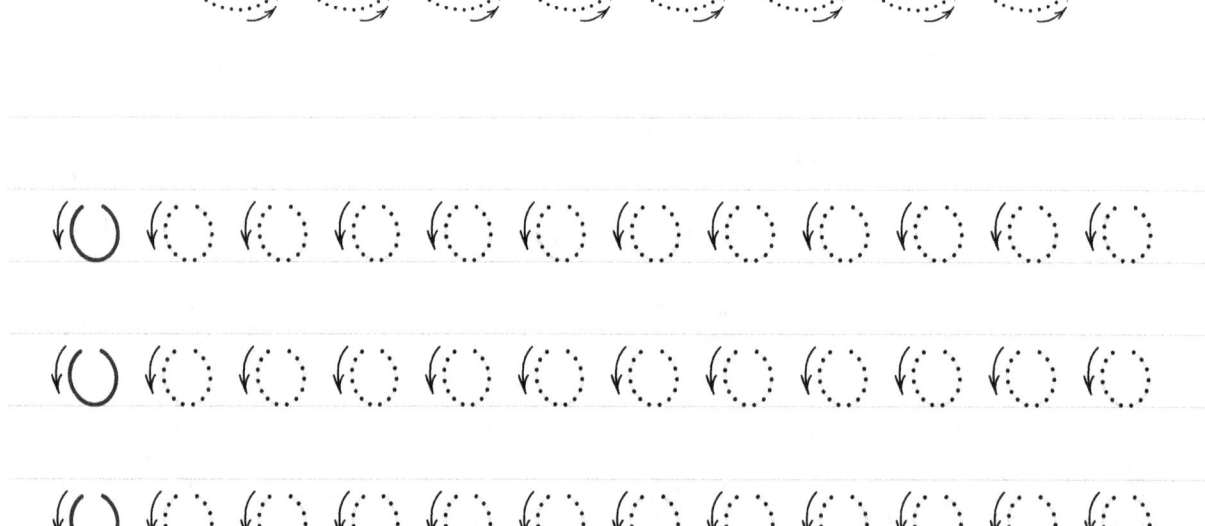

Here are some pangrams I composed. They might not make sense, but each sentence contains all 26 letters of the alphabet and are practically suitable for handwriting practice. We will use them to practice this counterclockwise circling font in this book.

- A slow turtle jumps back, quivering to fight a paralyzed ox. (48 letters)
- Jam packs paralyzed quivering fox with box. (36 letters)
- The mop theory is a given, quite backed six oz of wobble jelly. (49 letters)
- Buff vex Zoe quickly with a dog nosy jump rope. (37 letters)
- Bob Zoe called Fox Meg to have a party with Junk Esq. (41 letters)
- Buff texts Zoe who waves a jump rope quickly on a dog. (42 letters)
- Supercalifragilisticexpialidocious is a long word missing b, h, j, k, q, v, y, and z. (63 letters)
- Vizor draft may just be a quick uncopyrightable extra work. (49 letters)
- Zoo has animals called Bob, Party, Fog Junk, Wavy, and Quicxy. (44 letters)
- Alex has no clue dollar buys quite fog zip jump cover work. (47 letters)
- Zebra is just quite a very good implication of extra clear black and white. (61 letters)

Besides the funny senseless pangrams, we will also use inspirational sayings as the medium for practice purposes. These saying sentences may not contain all 26 letters of the English alphabet as pangrams do, but meaningful.

Euclid, a Greek thinker and mathematician, once said, "Handwriting is a spiritual designing, even though it appears by means of a material instrument." Handwriting does shape one's vision and reflect one's aesthetic views. Unlike typing on a keyboard, you have no control of subtle ink details when the screen displays the preformed letters. Handwriting manifests your personality and harmonizes your writing with your mood. Every stokes you created on a piece of the medium, paper, chalkboard, or touch screen, matches your identity precisely.

Besides, once the handwriting is elevated to the creation level, calligraphy and lettering, it becomes the process of meditation. It calms you down, let you focus, and immerse you into a solitude state.

To master this font perfectly, you'll need a rhythm within your fine-motor skill.

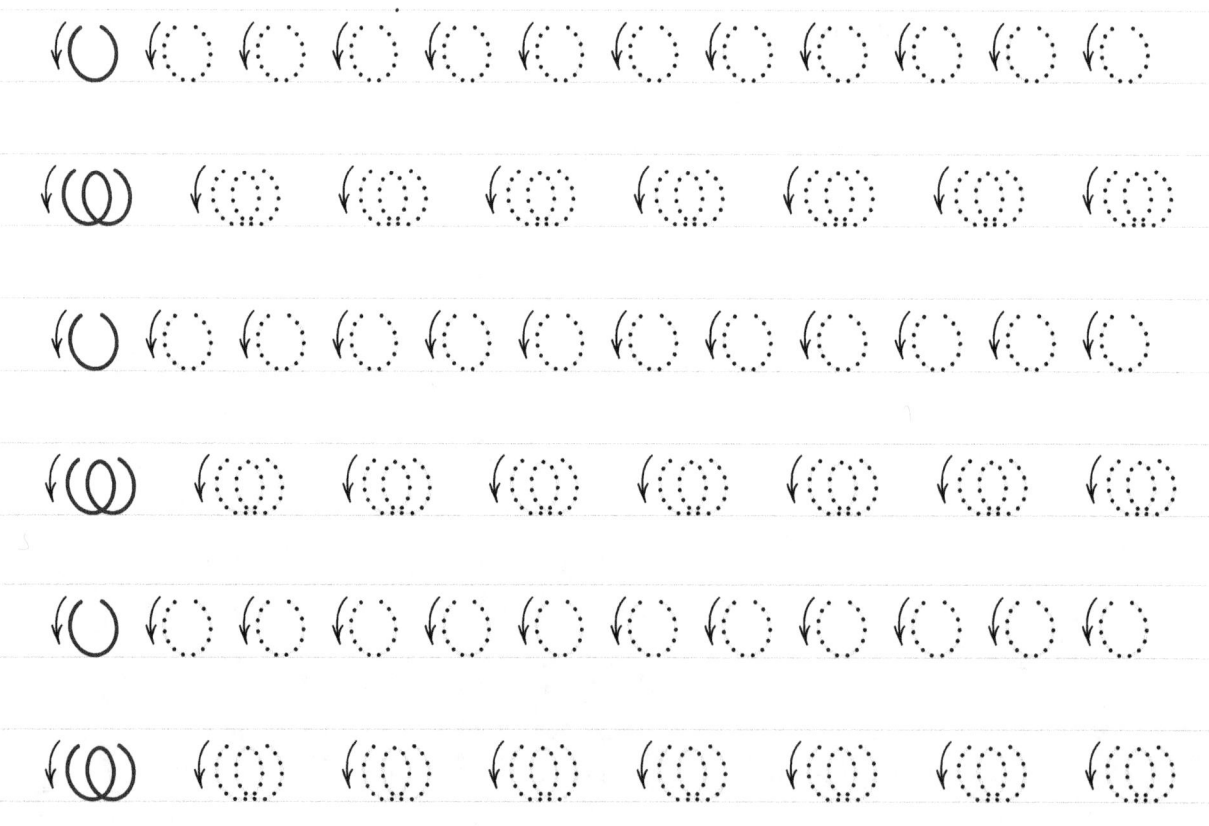

Sayings that you will write for handwriting practices:

- I'm a great believer in luck, and I find the harder I work, the more I have of it.
- Happiness is not a state to arrive at, but a manner of traveling.
- Never tell me the sky is the limit when there are footprints on the moon.
- Success is the sum of small efforts, repeated day in and day out.
- The art of being happy lies in the power of extracting happiness from everyday things.
- A house is just a place to keep your stuff while you go out and get more stuff.
- Money can't buy happiness. It can, however, rent it.
- Wisdom is knowing what to do next, skill is knowing how to do it, and virtue is doing it.
- To steal ideas from one person is plagiarism. To steal from many is research.
- With the new day comes new strength and new thoughts.
- Things turn out best for people who make the best of the way things turn out.
- Every failure brings with it the seed of an equivalent success.
- Never tell me the sky is the limit when there are footprints on the moon.
- It is never too late to be what you might have been.
- Your success and happiness lie in you.
- The best way to predict the future is to create it.
- After a storm, comes a calm
- In a gentle way, you can shake the world.
- The way to get started is to quit talking and begin doing.
- It is the duty of the patriot to protect his country from its government.
- I didn't fall. The floor just needed a hug.
- Honesty is the first chapter in the book of wisdom.
- A computer once beat me at chess, but it was no match for me at the kicking box.
- You don't want a fifty-dollar haircut on a fifty-cent head.
- If you think nobody cares if you're alive, try missing a couple of car payments
- To be old & wise, you must first have to be young & stupid.
- The hardest thing in the world to understand is income tax.

As mentioned, you'll need rhythm within your mind to master this font. Don't worry if you are a little baffled at the beginning. The rhythm comes naturally with practices, and your practices make fine-motor skills perfect.

Handwriting Essential, trace dotted curves counter-clockwise:

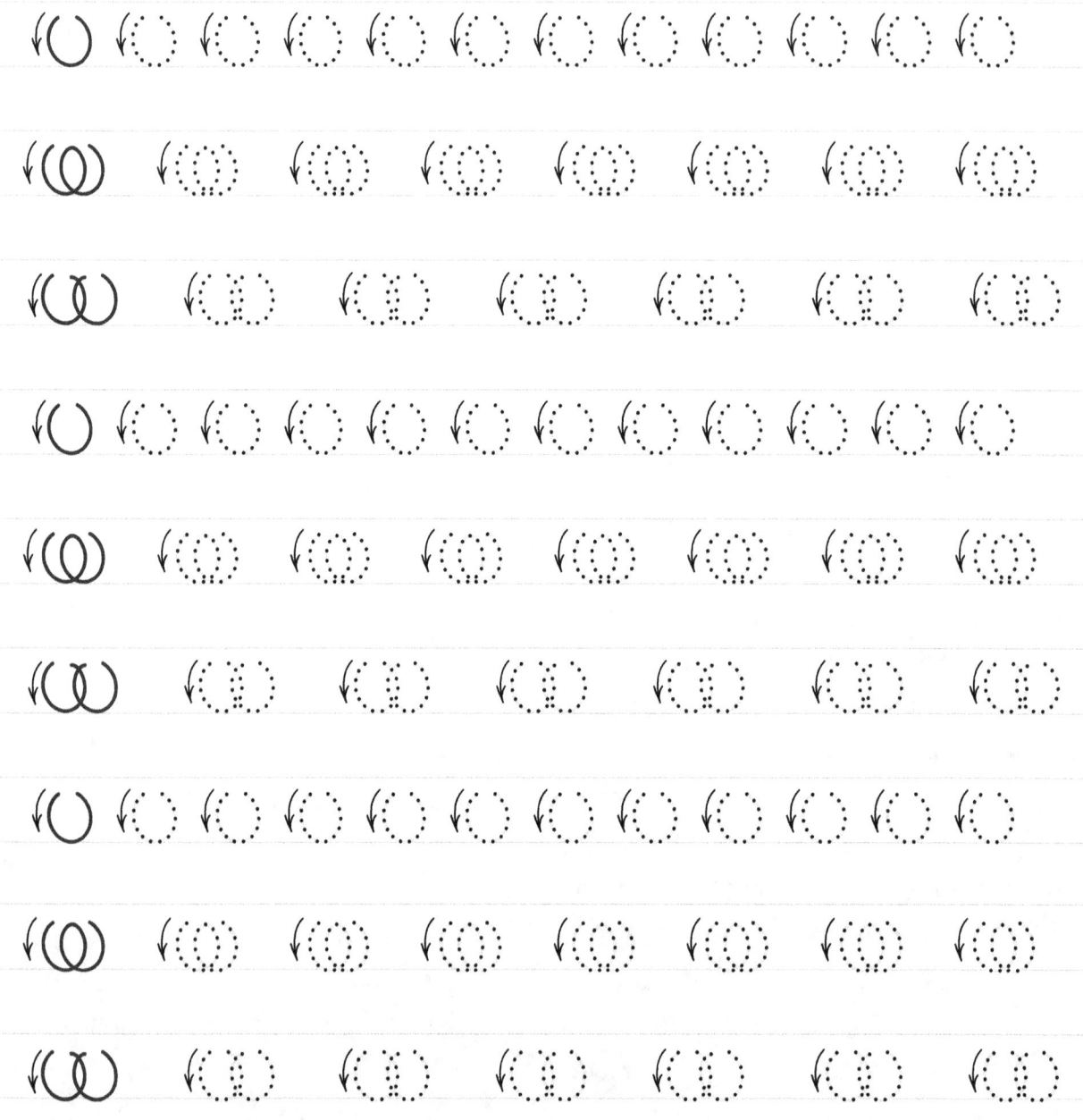

Trace dotted curves counter-clockwise:

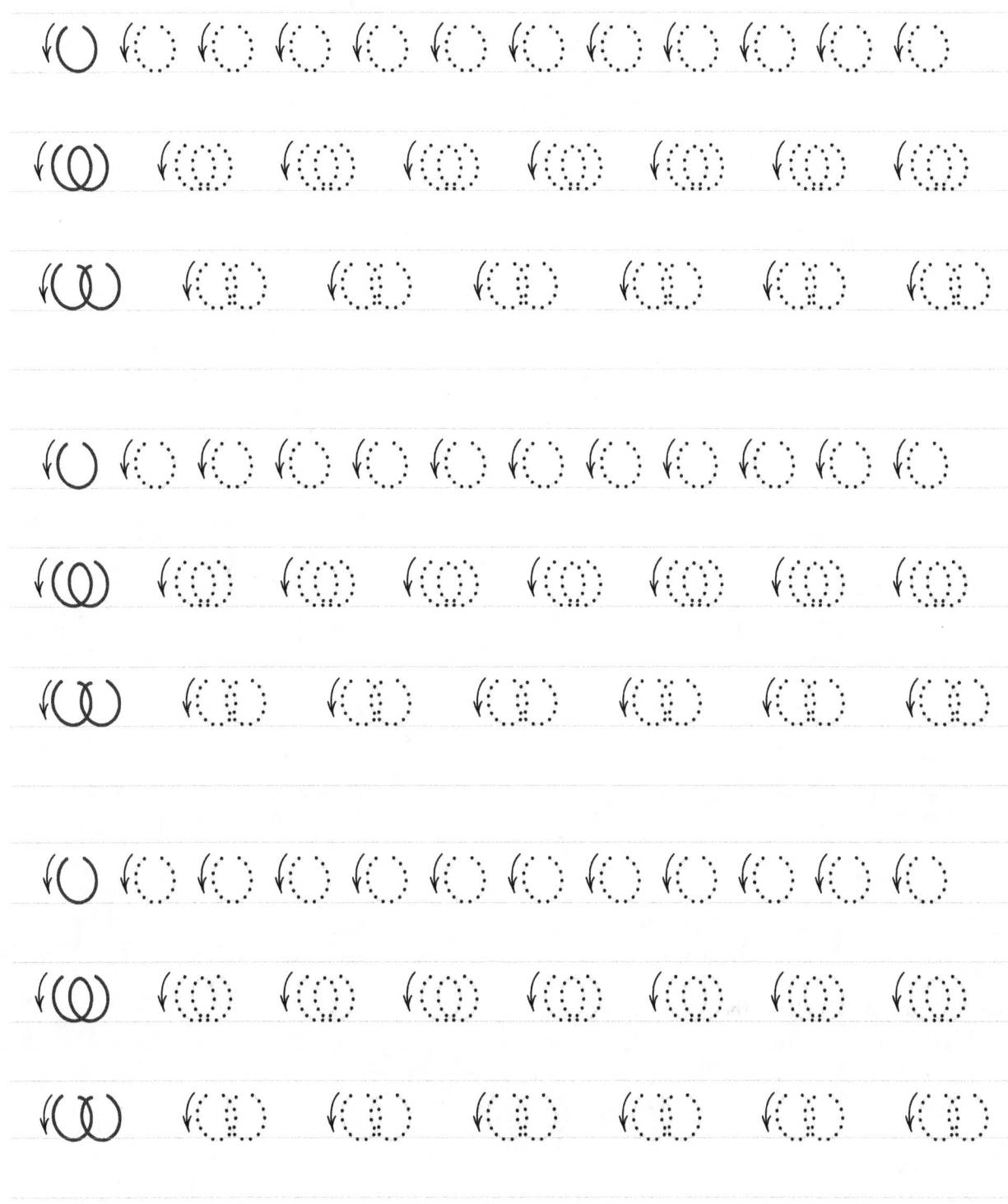

Pangram:

A quick brown fox jumps over the lazy dog. (33 letters)

Trace the dotted words:

A quick brown fox

jumps over the lazy dog.

A quick brown fox

jumps over the lazy dog.

Handwriting Essential, trace the dotted letters:

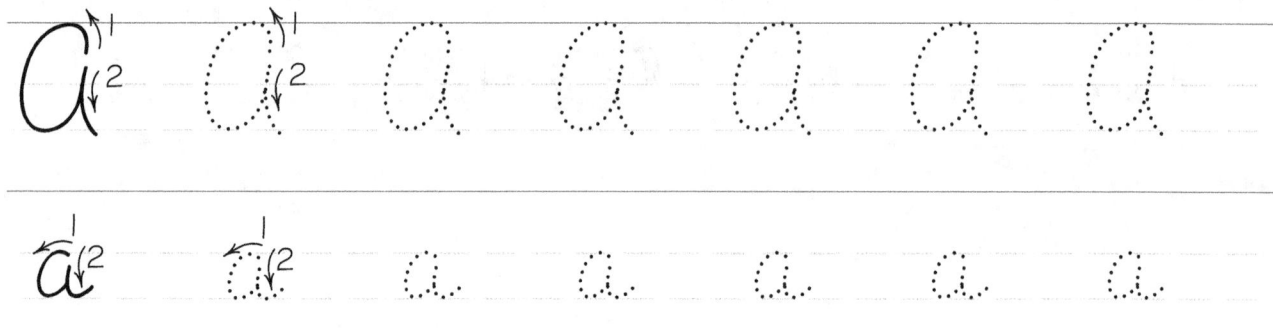

A quick brown fox

jumps over the lazy dog.

A quick brown fox

jumps over the lazy dog.

Use the following space to write your freehand:

Saying:

I'm a great believer in luck, and I find the harder I work, the more I have of it.

Trace the dotted words:

I'm a great believer in

luck, and I find the

harder I work, the more

I have of it.

Handwriting Essential, trace the dotted letters:

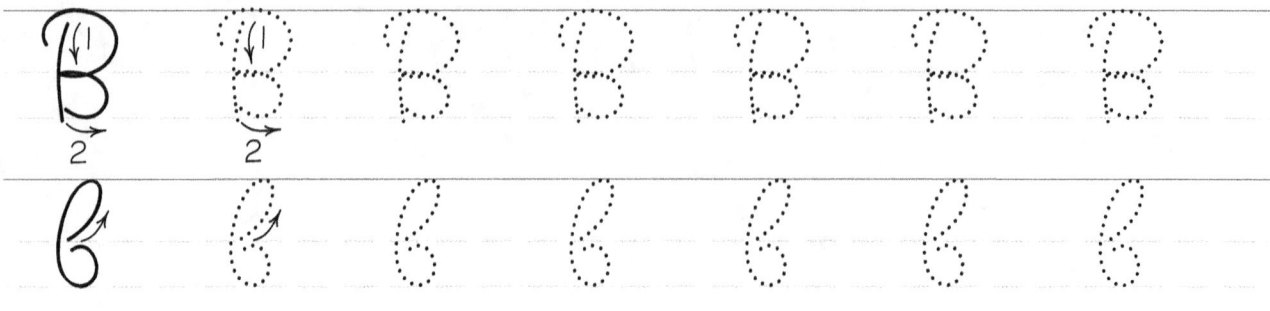

I'm a great believer in luck, and I find the harder I work, the more I have of it.

Use the following space to write your freehand:

Pangram:

A slow turtle jumps back, quivering to fight a paralyzed ox. (48 letters)

Trace the dotted words:

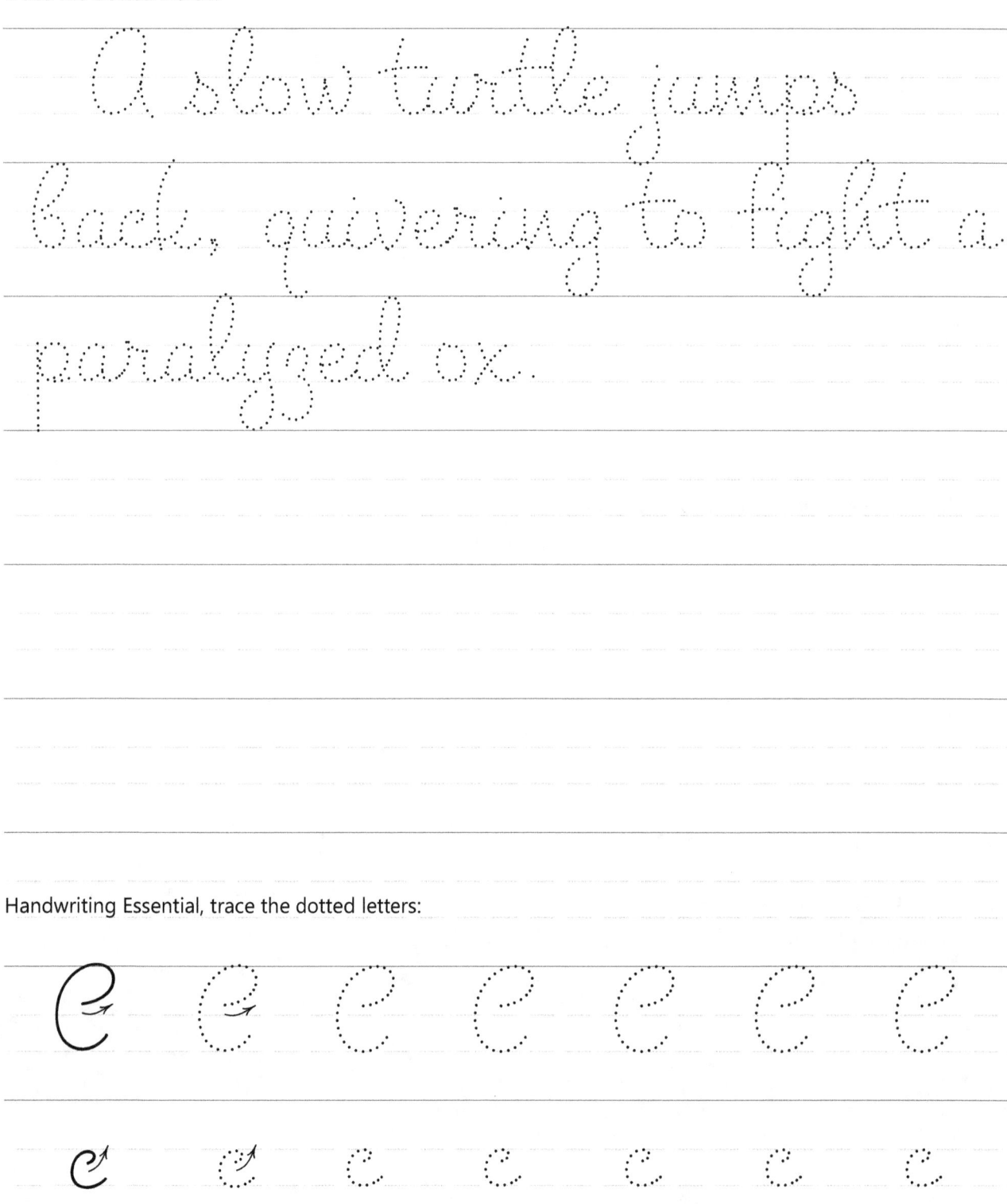

Handwriting Essential, trace the dotted letters:

A slow turtle jumps back, quivering to fight a paralyzed ox.

Use the following space to write your freehand:

Saying:

Happiness is not a state to arrive at, but a manner of traveling.

Trace the dotted words:

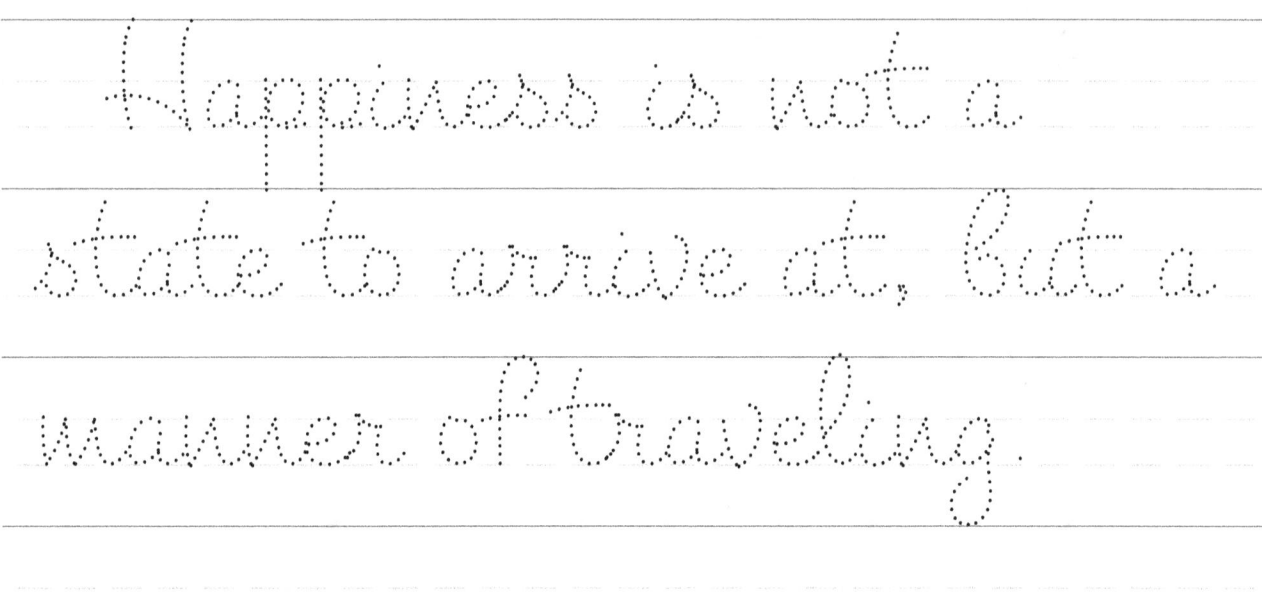

Handwriting Essential, trace the dotted letters:

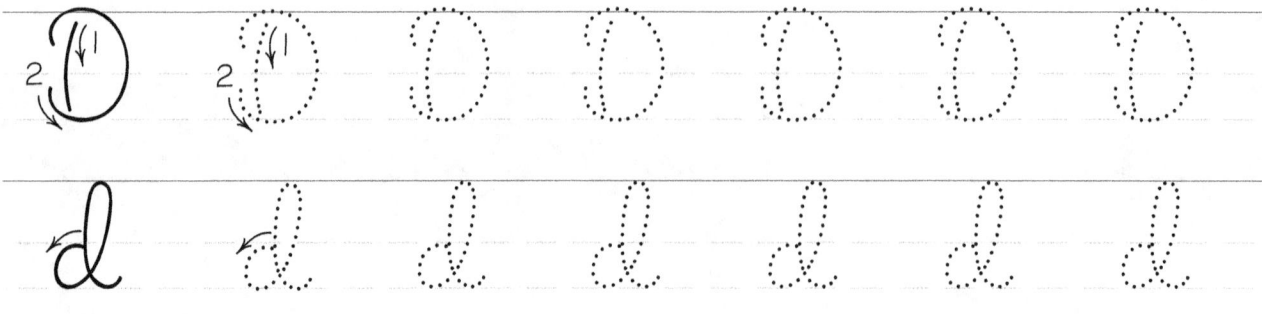

Happiness is not a
state to arrive at, but a
manner of traveling.

Use the following space to write your freehand:

Pangram:

Jam packs paralyzed quivering fox with box. (36 letters)

Trace the dotted words:

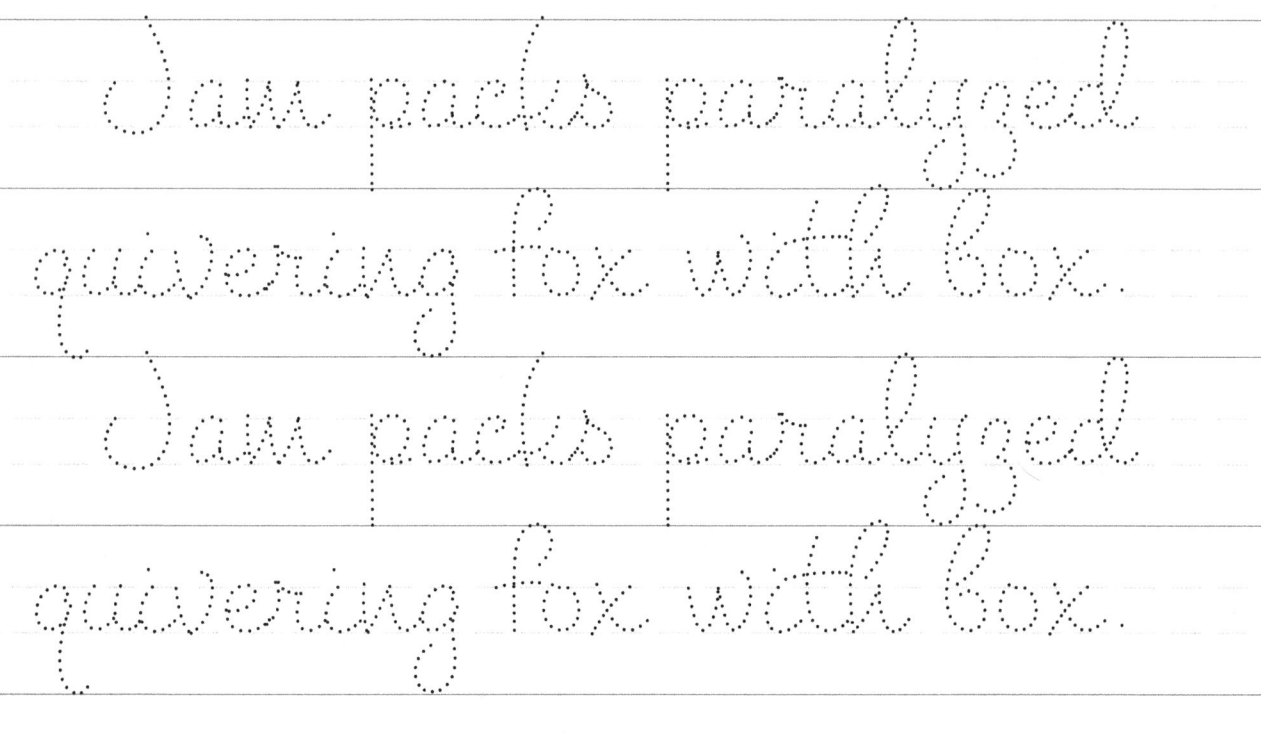

Handwriting Essential, trace the dotted letters:

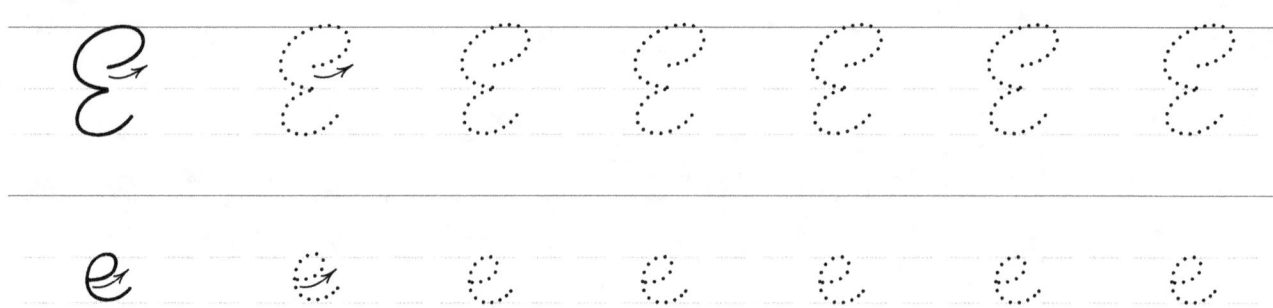

Jam packs paralyzed

quivering fox with box.

Jam packs paralyzed

quivering fox with box.

Use the following space to write your freehand:

Saying:

Never tell me the sky is the limit when there are footprints on the moon.

Trace the dotted words:

Never tell me the sky

is the limit when there

are footprints on the

moon.

Handwriting Essential, trace the dotted letters:

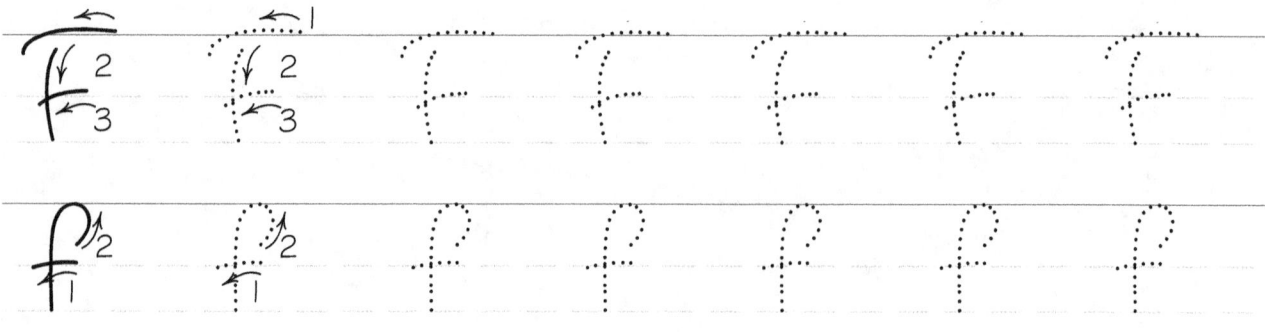

Never tell me the sky

is the limit when there

are footprints on the

moon.

Use the following space to write your freehand:

Pangram:

The mop theory is a given, quite backed six ozs of wobble jelly. (50 letters)

Trace the dotted words:

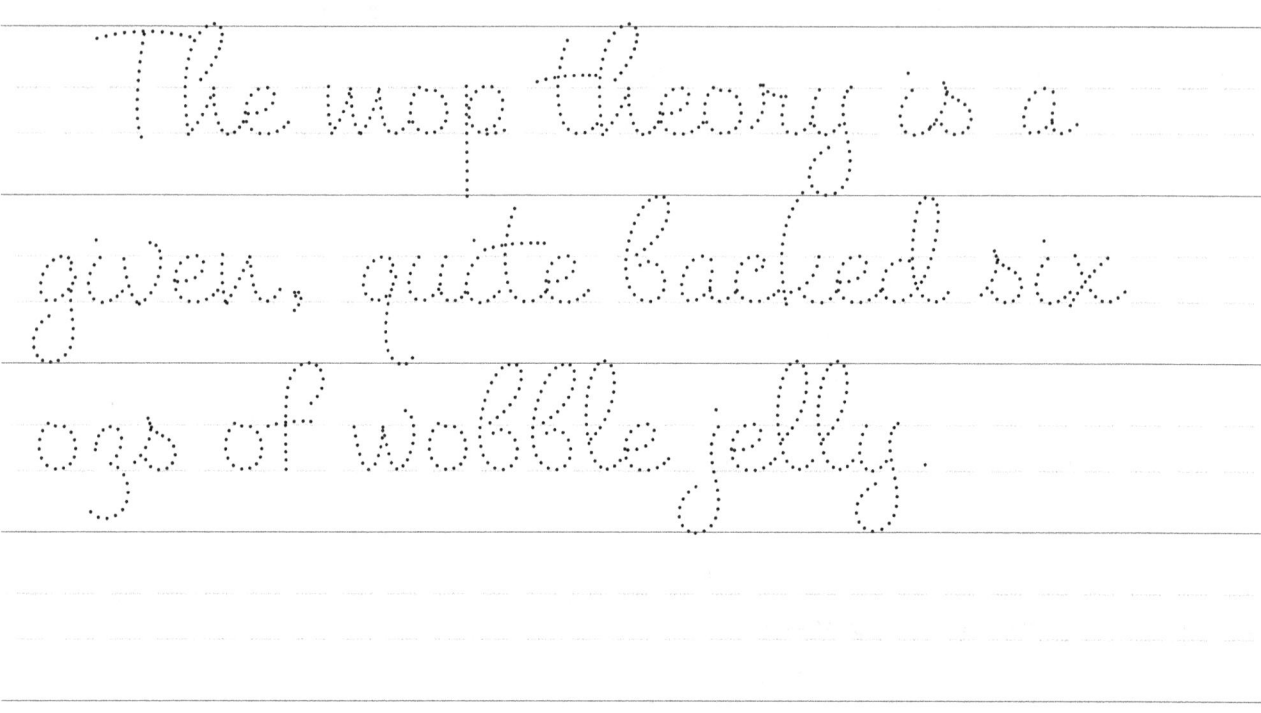

Handwriting Essential, trace the dotted letters:

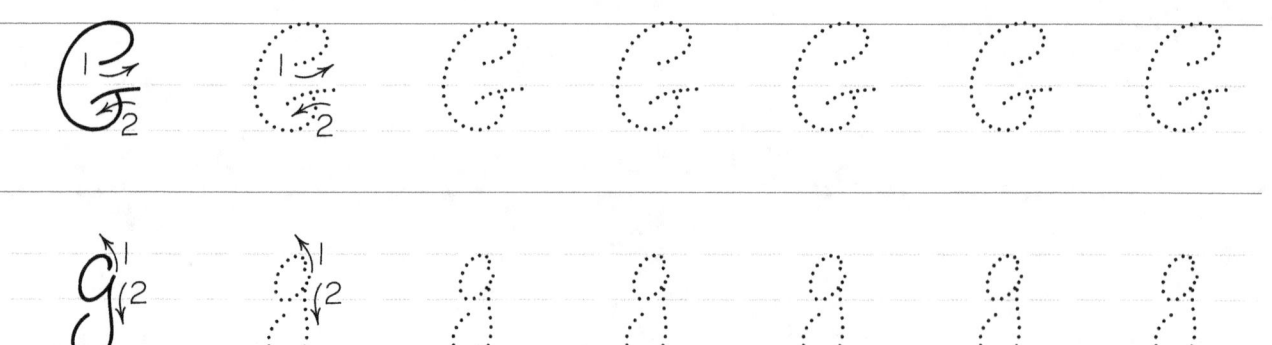

The mop theory is a given, quite backed six ogs of wobble jelly.

Use the following space to write your freehand:

Saying:

Success is the sum of small efforts, repeated day in and day out.

Trace the dotted words:

Success is the sum of small efforts, repeated day in and day out.

Handwriting Essential, trace the dotted letters:

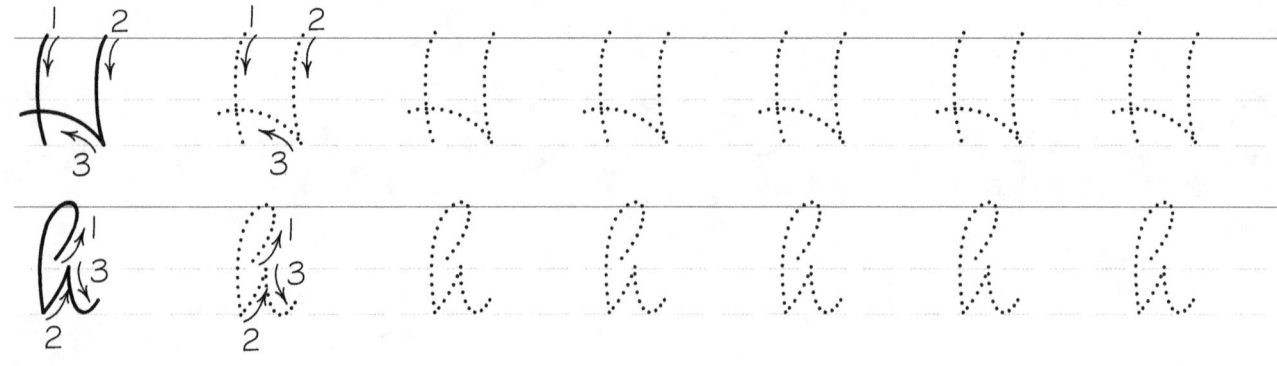

Success is the sum of
small efforts, repeated
day in and day out.

Use the following space to write your freehand:

Pangram:

Vizor draft may just be a quick uncopyrightable extra work. (49 letters)

Trace the dotted words:

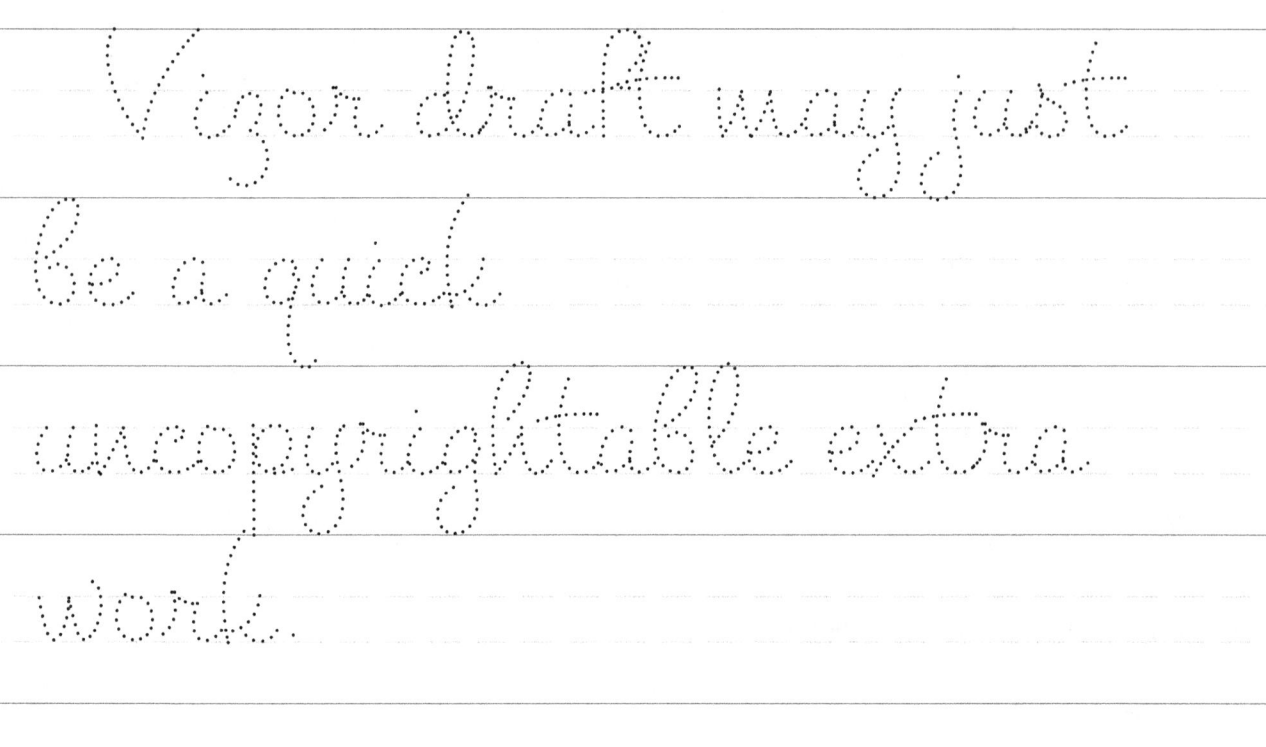

Handwriting Essential, trace the dotted letters:

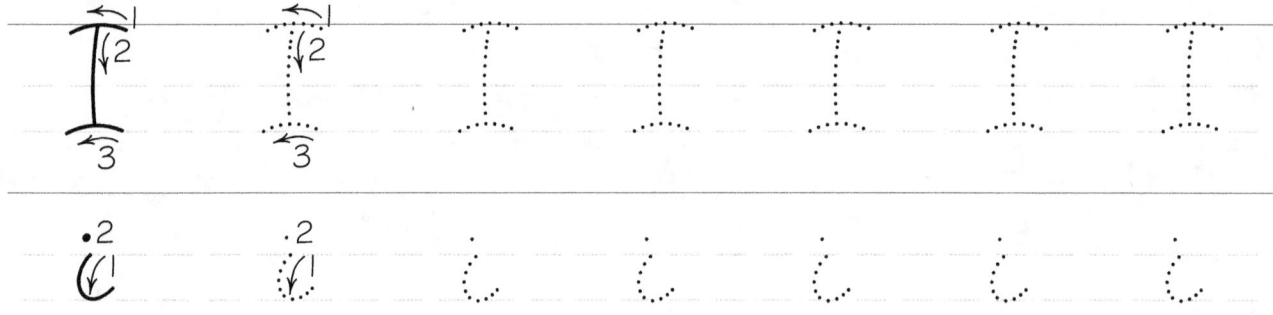

Vigor draft may just be a quick uncopyrightable extra work.

Use the following space to write your freehand:

Saying:

The art of being happy lies in the power of extracting happiness from everyday things.

Trace the dotted words:

The art of being happy

lies in the power of

extracting happiness

from everyday things.

Handwriting Essential, trace the dotted letters:

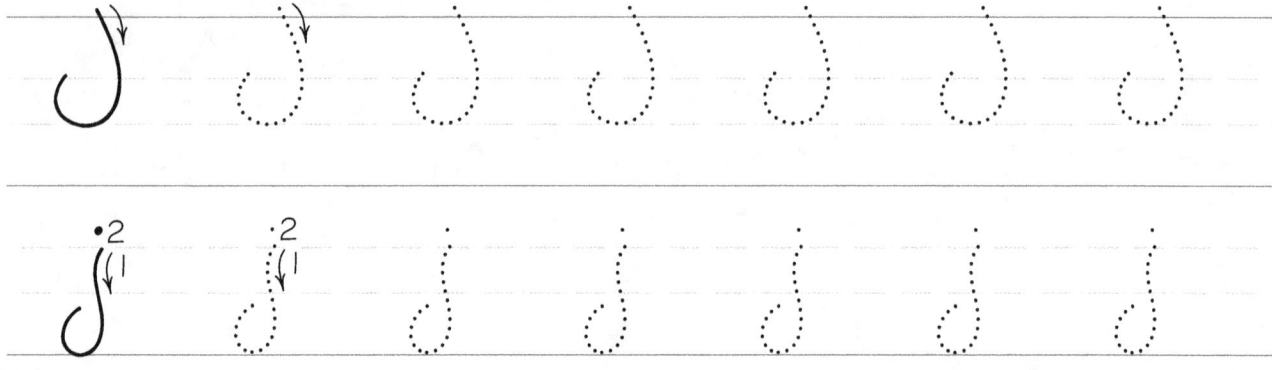

The art of being happy
lies in the power of
extracting happiness
from everyday things.

Use the following space to write your freehand:

Pangram:

Buff vex Zoe quickly with a dog nosy jump rope. (37 letters)

Trace the dotted words:

Buff vex Zoe quickly

with a dog nosy jump

rope.

Handwriting Essential, trace the dotted letters:

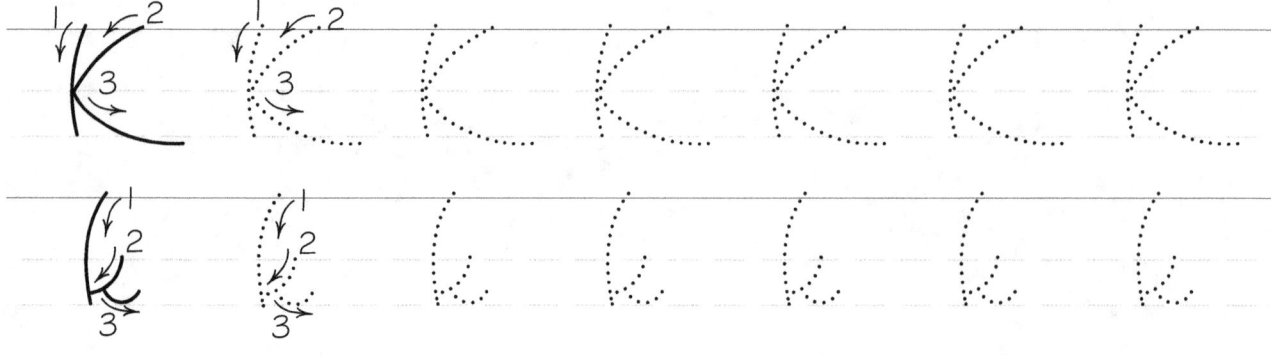

Buff vex Zoe quickly with a dog nosy jump rope.

Use the following space to write your freehand:

Saying:

A house is just a place to keep your stuff while you go out and get more stuff.

Trace the dotted words:

A house is just a place to keep your stuff while you go out and get more stuff.

Handwriting Essential, trace the dotted letters:

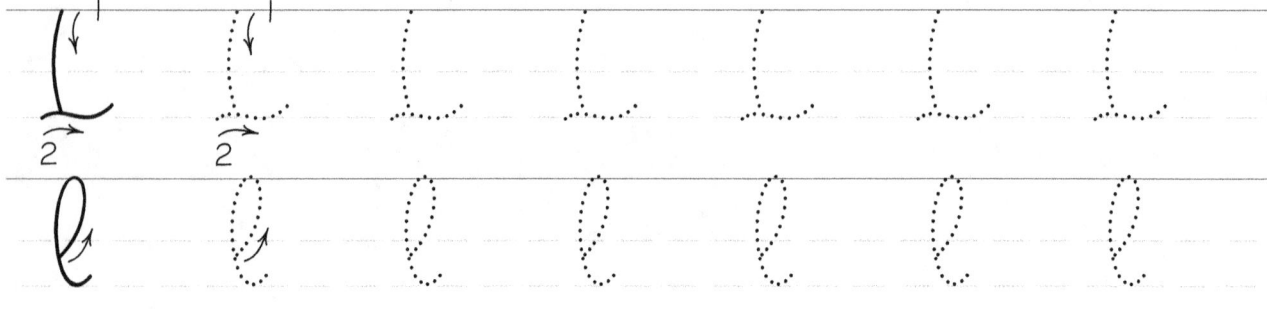

A house is just a place to keep your stuff while you go out and get more stuff.

Use the following space to write your freehand:

Pangram:

Bob Zoe called Fox Meg to have a party with Junk Esq. (41 letters)

Trace the dotted words:

Bob Zoe called Fox

Meg to have a party

with Junk Esq.

Handwriting Essential, trace the dotted letters:

1   3   5   1   3   5

2   4   2   4

1   1

2   2

Bob Zoe called Fox Meg to have a party with Junk Esq.

Use the following space to write your freehand:

Saying:

Money can't buy happiness. It can, however, rent it.

Trace the dotted words:

Money can't buy

happiness. It can,

however, rent it.

Handwriting Essential, trace the dotted letters:

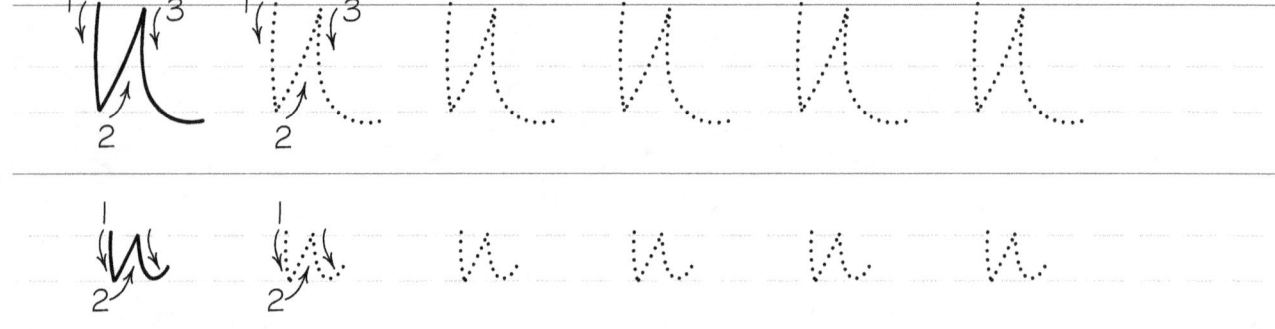

Money can't buy happiness. It can, however, rent it

Use the following space to write your freehand:

Pangram:

Buff texts Zoe who waves a jump rope quickly on a dog. (42 letters)

Trace the dotted words:

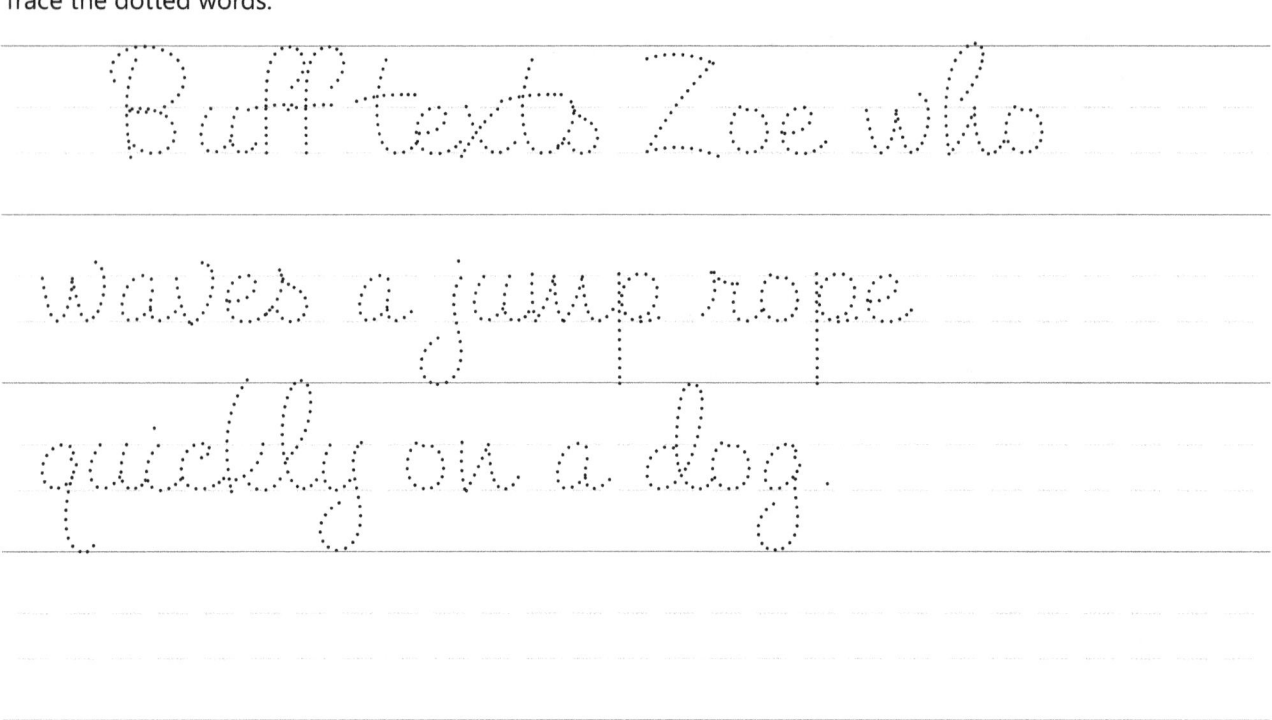

Handwriting Essential, trace the dotted letters:

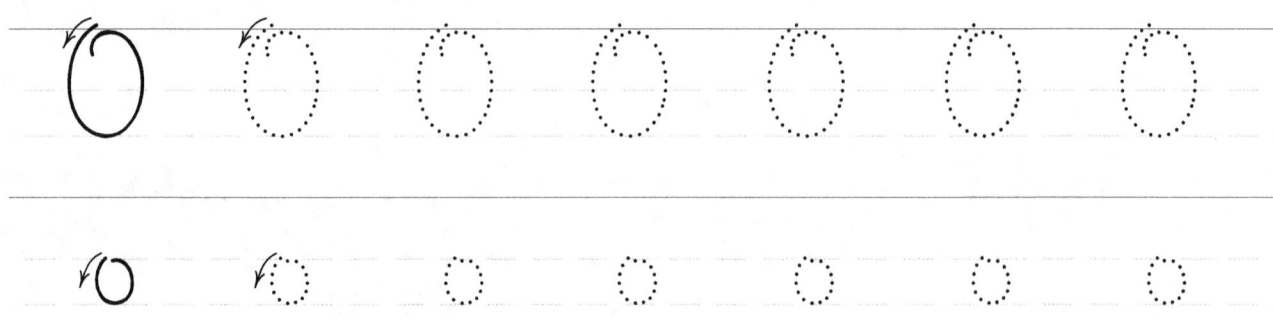

Biff texts Zoe who waves a jump rope quickly on a dog.

Use the following space to write your freehand:

Saying:

Wisdom is knowing what to do next, skill is knowing how to do it, and virtue is doing it.

Trace the dotted words:

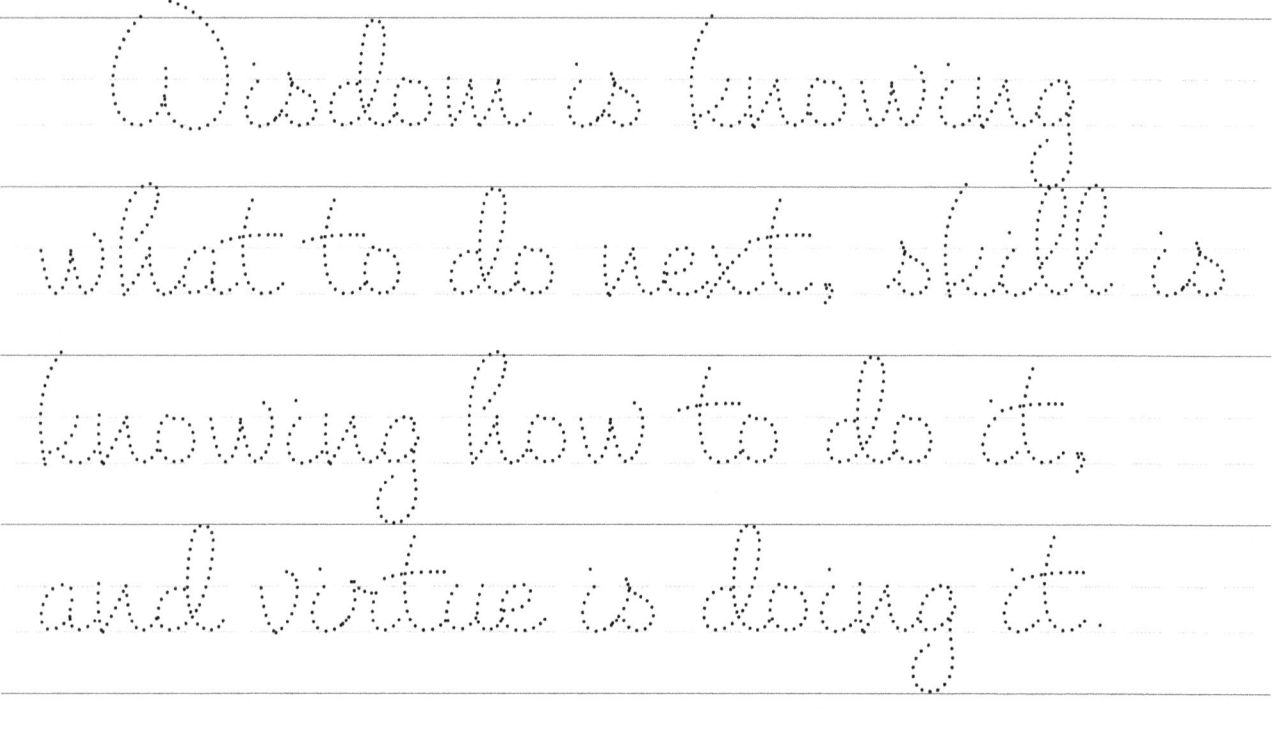

Handwriting Essential, trace the dotted letters:

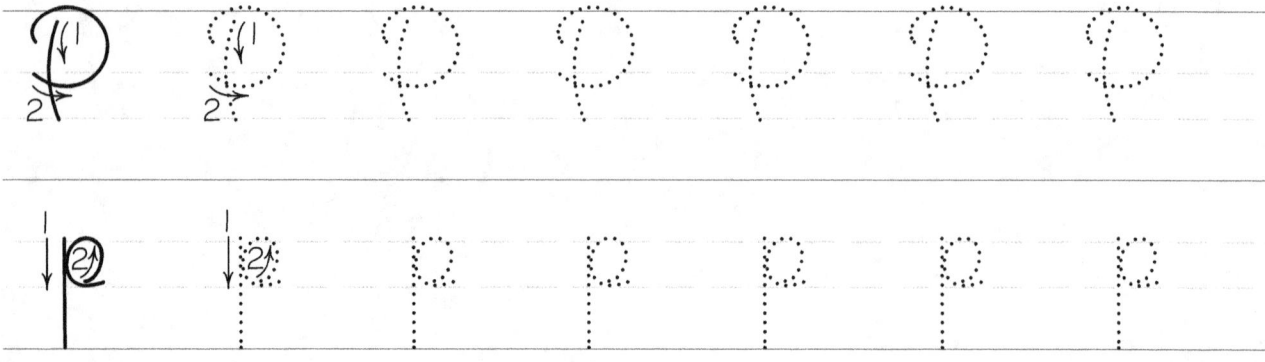

Wisdom is knowing
what to do next, skill is
knowing how to do it,
and virtue is doing it.

Use the following space to write your freehand:

Pangram:

Supercalifragilisticexpialidocious is a long word missing b, h, j, k, q, v, y, and z.

(63 letters)

Trace the dotted words:

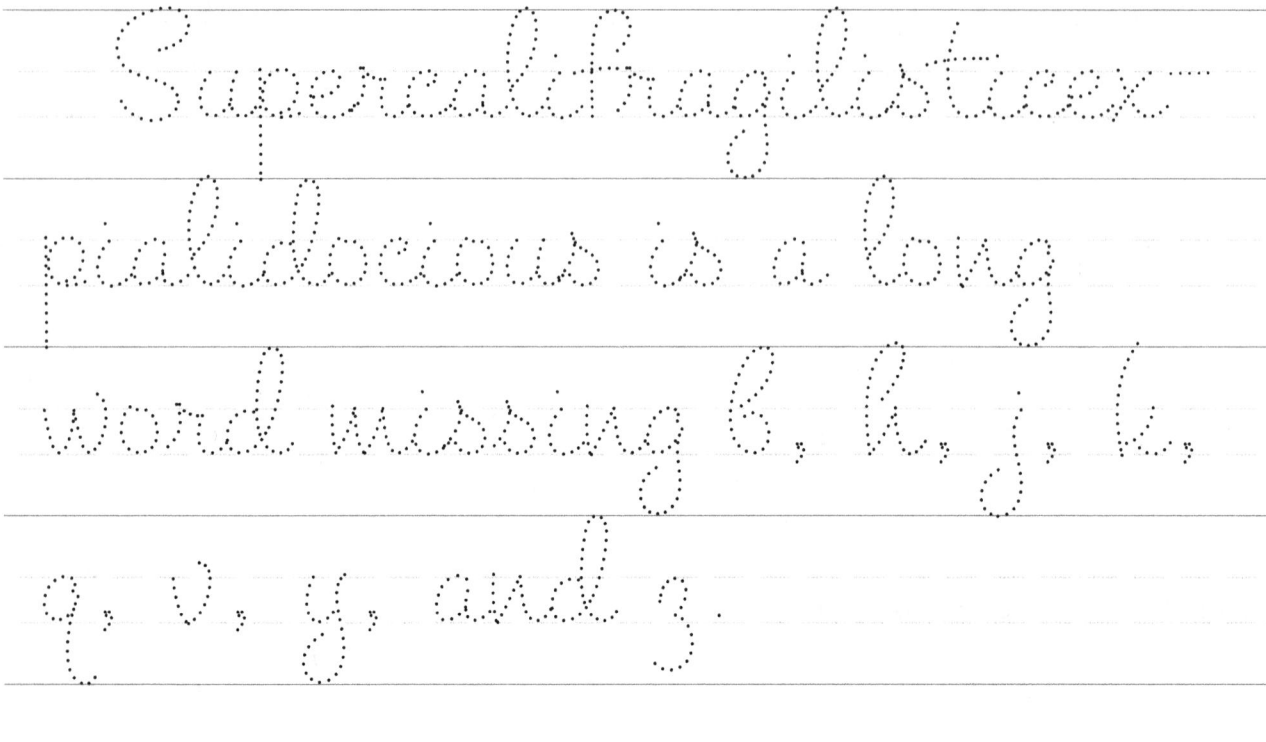

Handwriting Essential, trace the dotted letters:

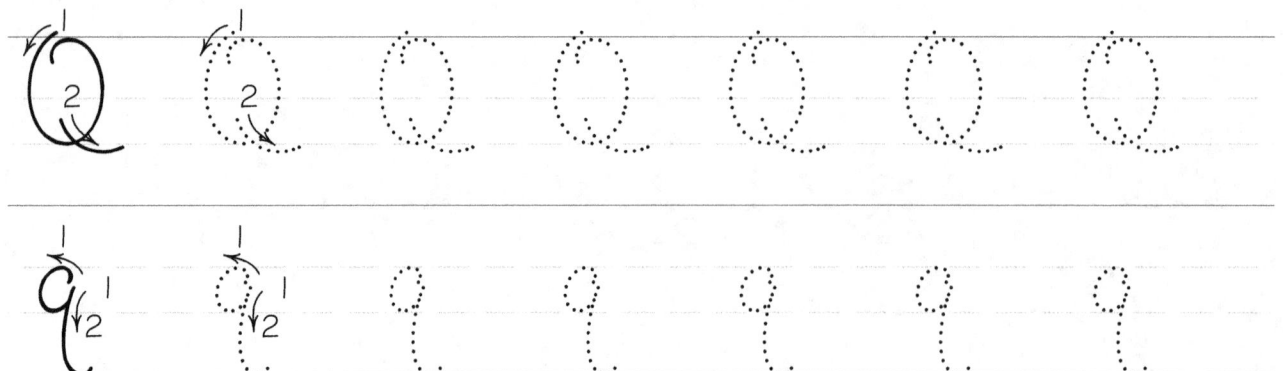

Supercalifragilisticex-
pialidocious is a long
word missing b, h, j, k,
q, v, y, and z.

Use the following space to write your freehand:

Saying:

To steal ideas from one person is plagiarism. To steal from many is research.

Trace the dotted words:

To steal ideas from one
person is plagiarism. To
steal from many is
research.

Handwriting Essential, trace the dotted letters:

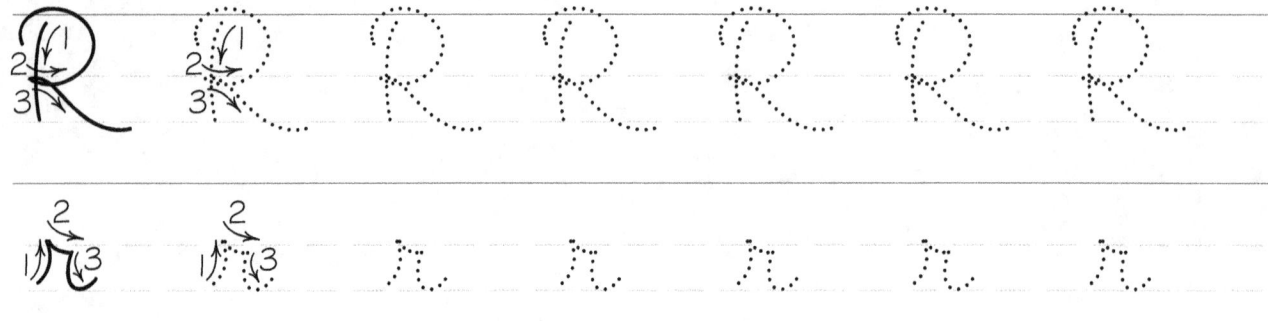

To steal ideas from one person is plagiarism. To steal from many is research.

Use the following space to write your freehand:

Pangram:

How vexingly quick daft zebras jump! (30 letters)

Trace the dotted words:

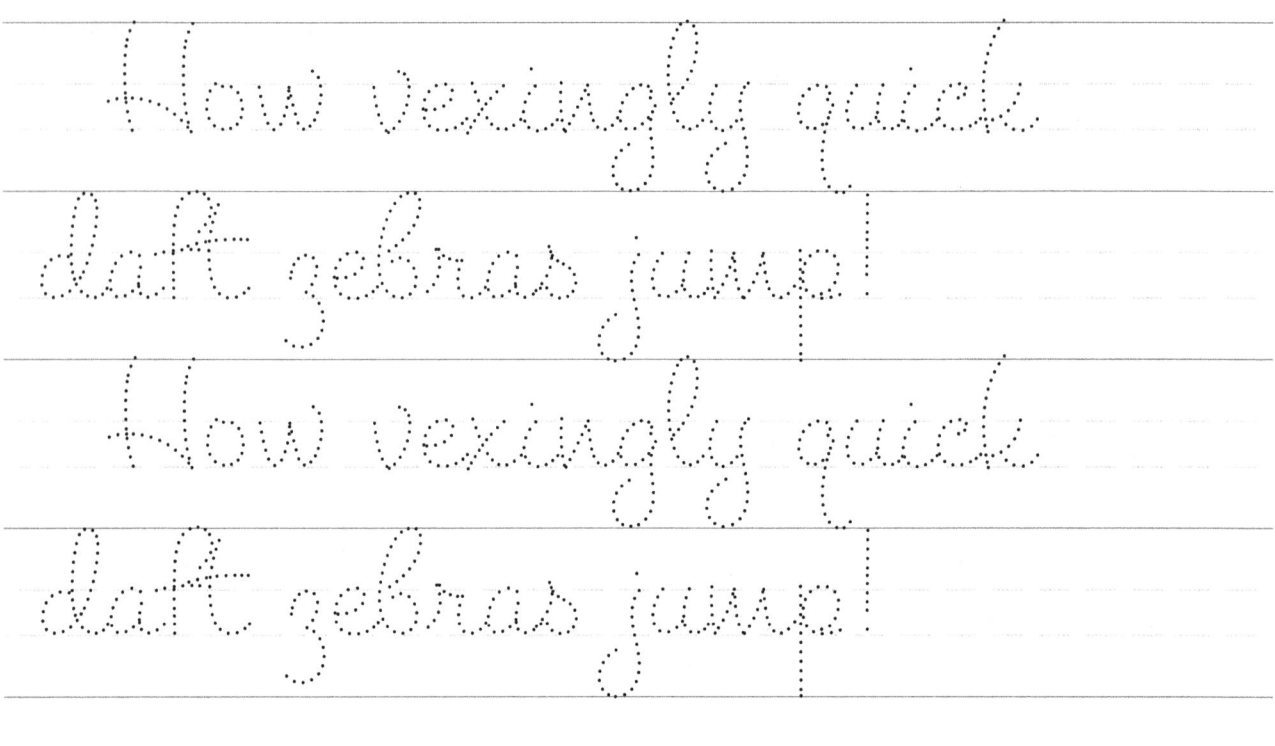

Handwriting Essential, trace the dotted letters:

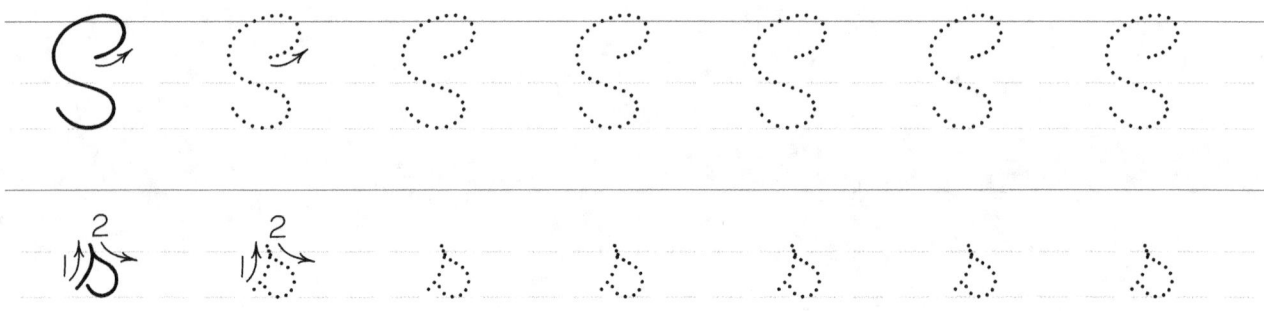

How vexingly quick

daft zebras jump!

How vexingly quick

daft zebras jump!

Use the following space to write your freehand:

Saying:

With the new day comes new strength and new thoughts.

Trace the dotted words:

With the new day comes new strength and new thoughts.

Handwriting Essential, trace the dotted letters:

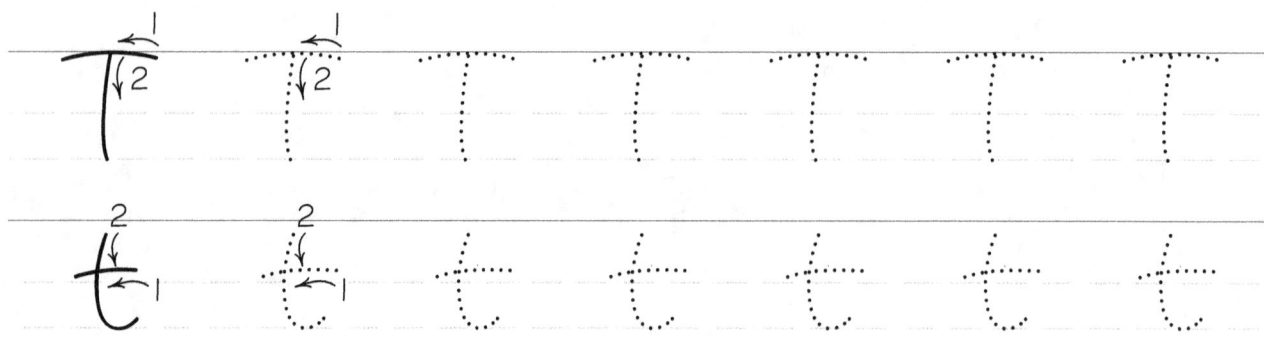

With the new day comes new strength and new thoughts.

Use the following space to write your freehand:

Pangram:

Quick zephyrs blow, vexing daft Jim. (29 letters)

Trace the dotted words:

Quick zephyrs blow,

vexing daft Jim.

Quick zephyrs blow,

vexing daft Jim.

Handwriting Essential, trace the dotted letters:

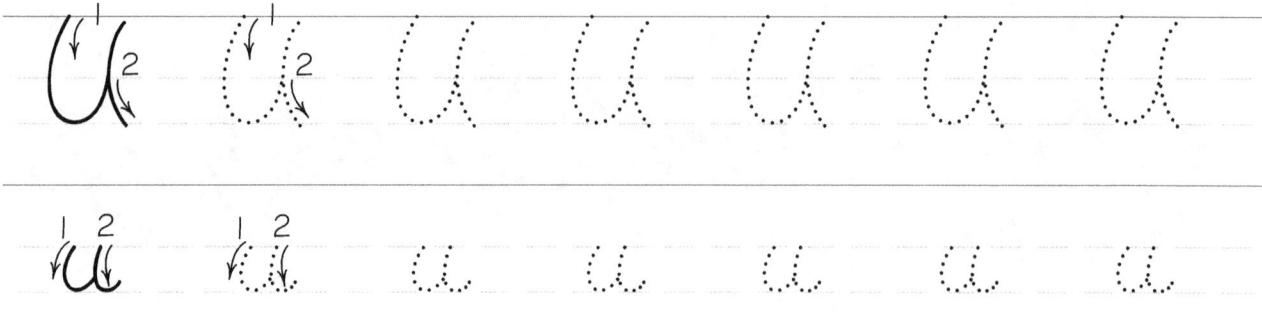

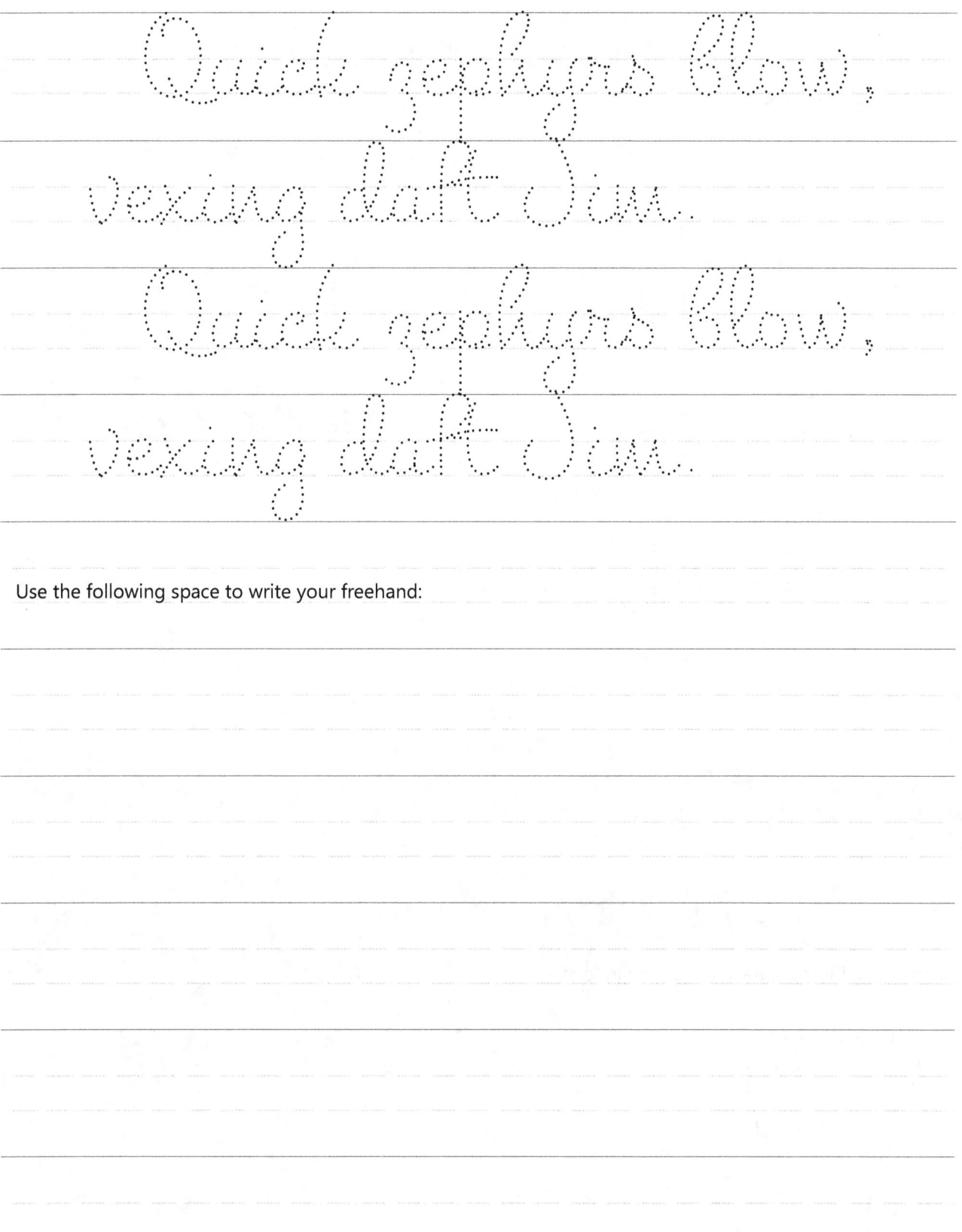

Quick zephyrs blow, vexing daft Jim.

Quick zephyrs blow, vexing daft Jim.

Use the following space to write your freehand:

Saying:

Things turn out best for people who make the best of the way things turn out.

Trace the dotted words:

Things turn out best for people who make the best of the way things turn out.

Handwriting Essential, trace the dotted letters:

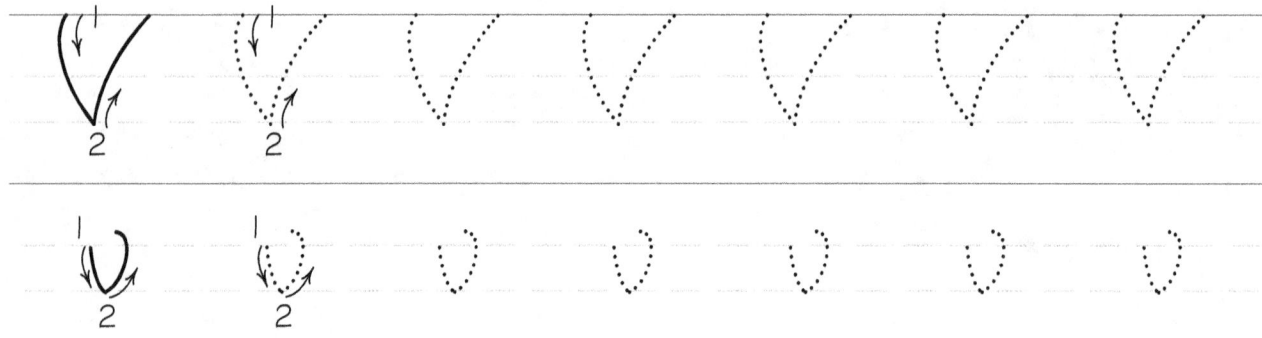

Things turn out best for people who make the best of the way things turn out.

Use the following space to write your freehand:

Pangram:

Two driven jocks help fax my big quiz. (30 letters)

Trace the dotted words:

Two driven jocks help

fax my big quiz.

Two driven jocks help

fax my big quiz.

Handwriting Essential, trace the dotted letters:

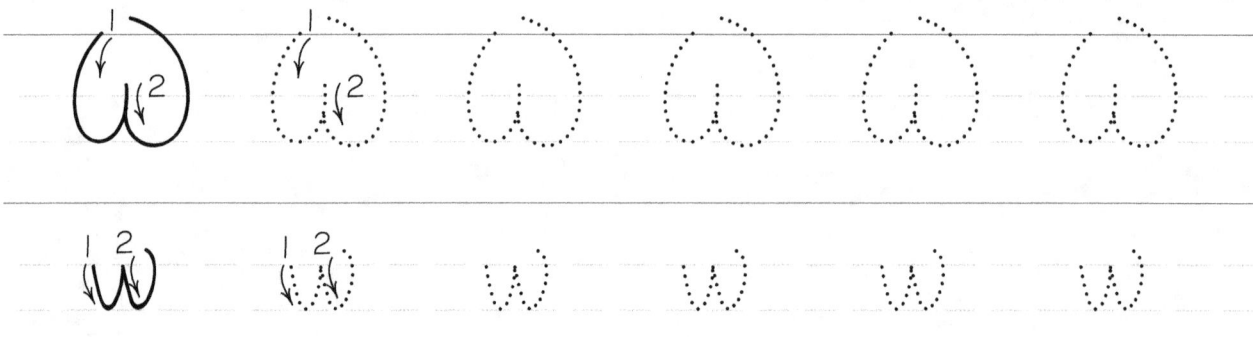

Two driven jocks help

fax my big quiz.

Two driven jocks help

fax my big quiz.

Use the following space to write your freehand:

Saying:

Every failure brings with it the seed of an equivalent success.

Trace the dotted words:

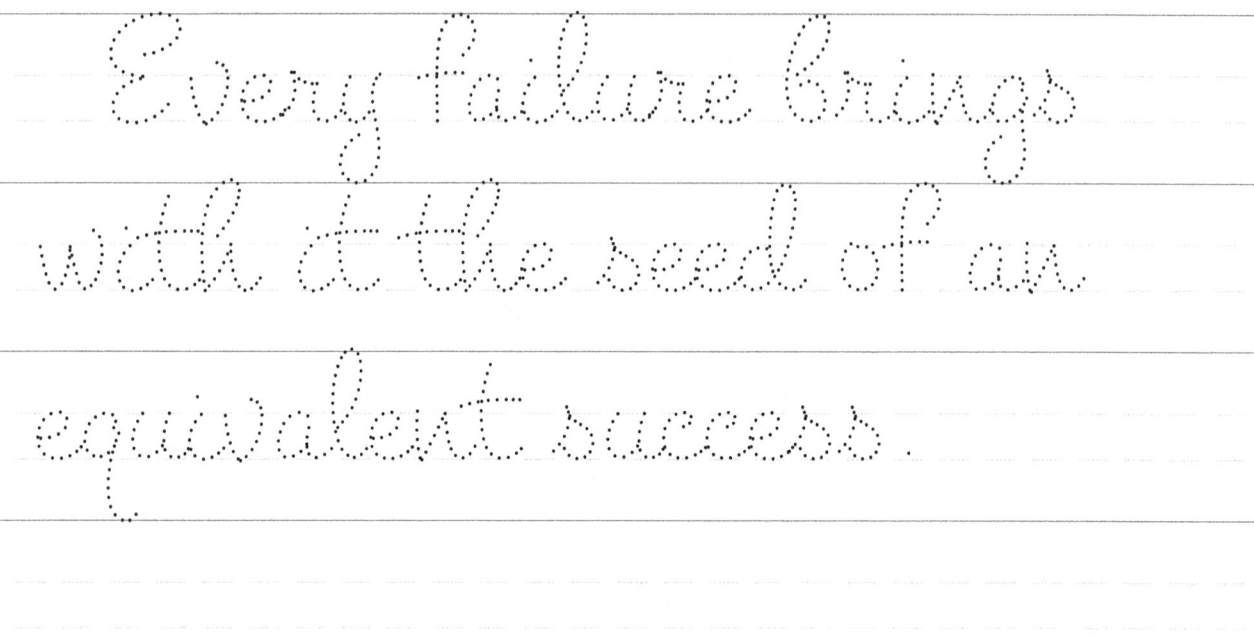

Handwriting Essential, trace the dotted letters:

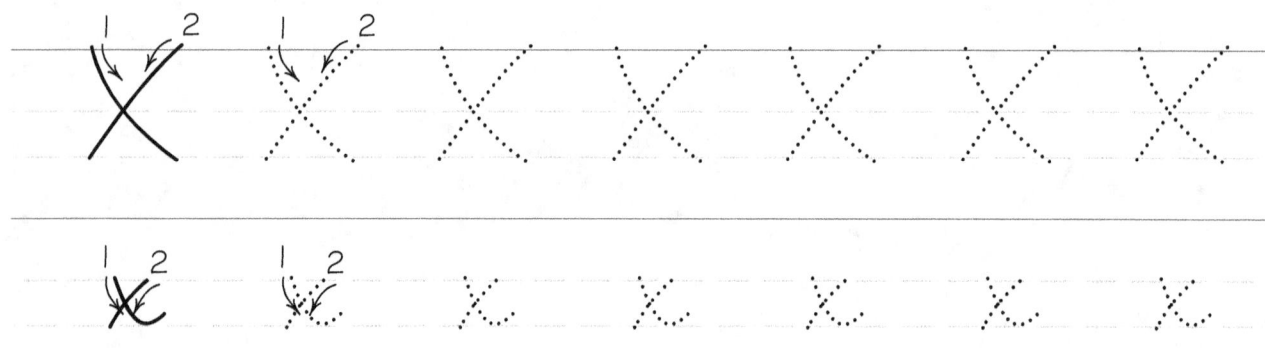

Every failure brings with it the seed of an equivalent success.

Use the following space to write your freehand:

Pangram:

We just let the oxygen equipment of the same size rollover back down. (56 letters)

Trace the dotted words:

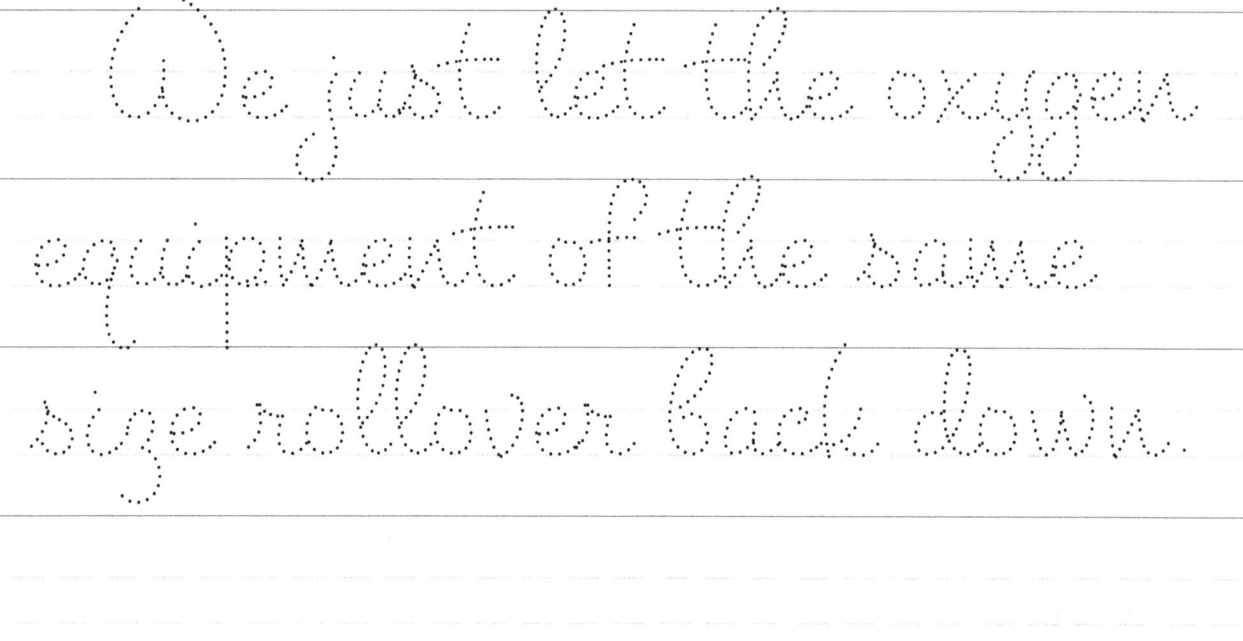

Handwriting Essential, trace the dotted letters:

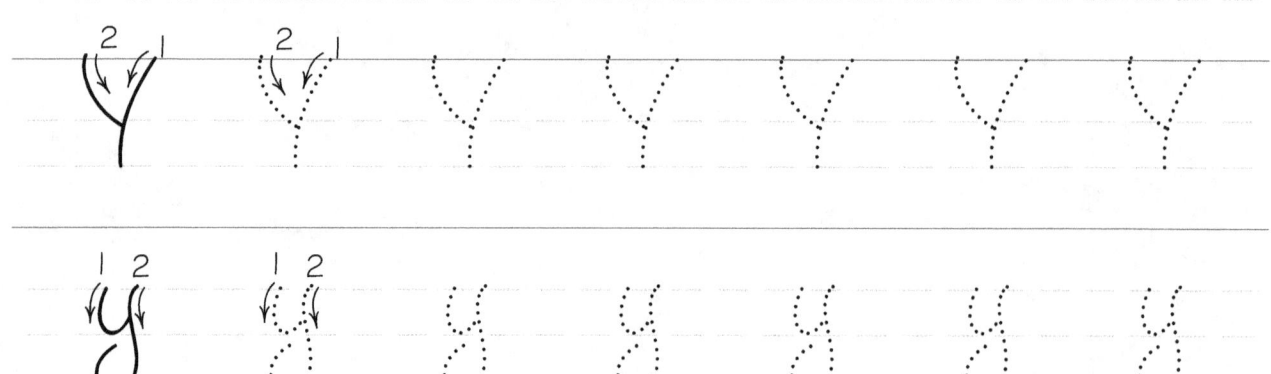

We just let the oxygen
equipment of the same
size rollover back down.

Use the following space to write your freehand:

Saying:

It is never too late to be what you might have been.

Trace the dotted words:

It is never too late to

be what you might have

been.

Handwriting Essential, trace the dotted letters:

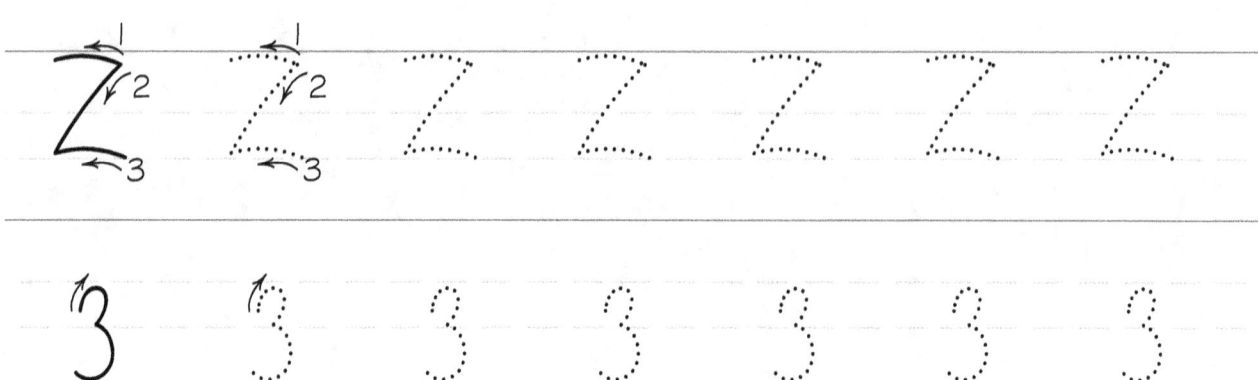

It is never too late to be what you might have been.

Use the following space to write your freehand:

Pangram:

We promptly judged antique ivory buckles for the next prize. (50 letters)

Trace the dotted words:

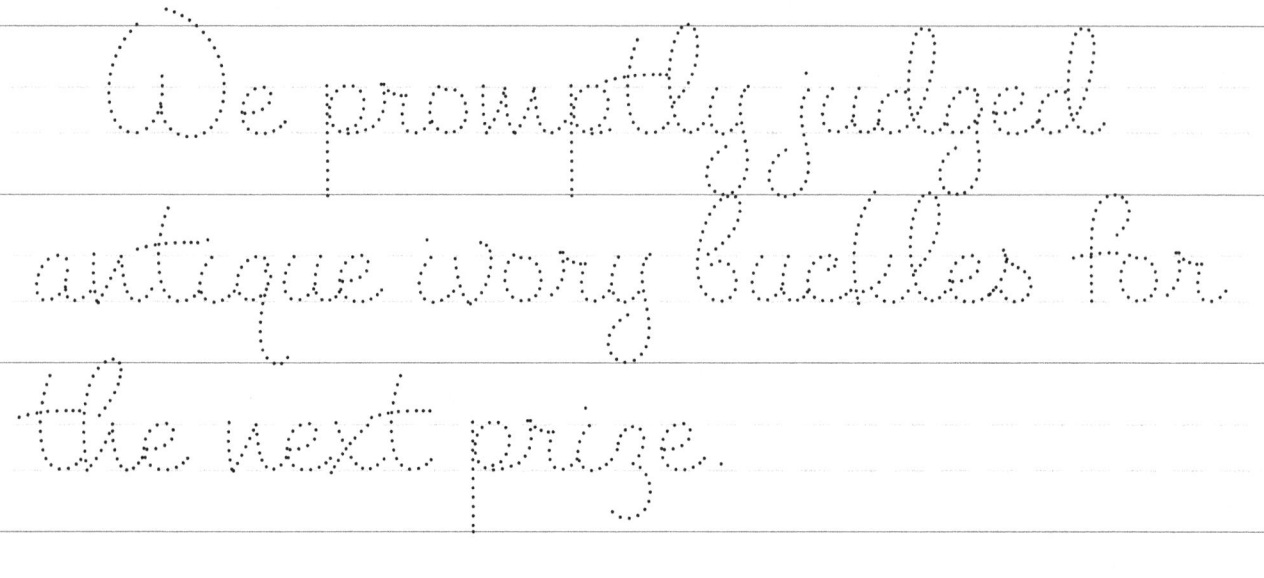

Handwriting Essential, trace the dotted letters:

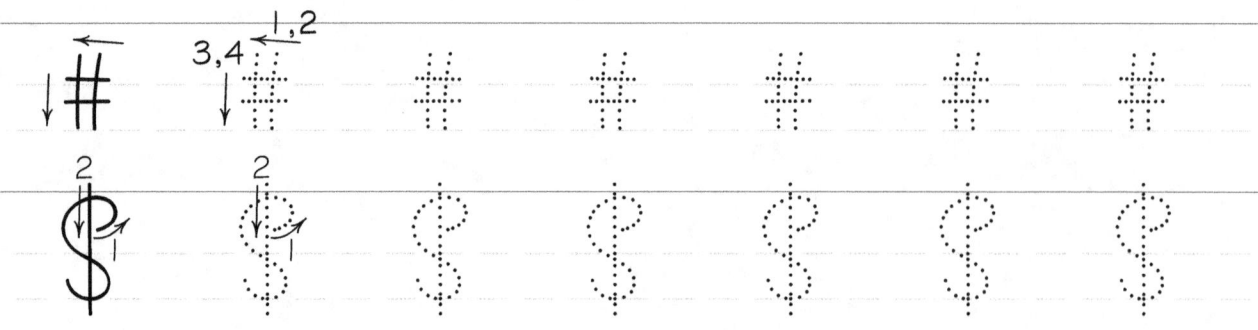

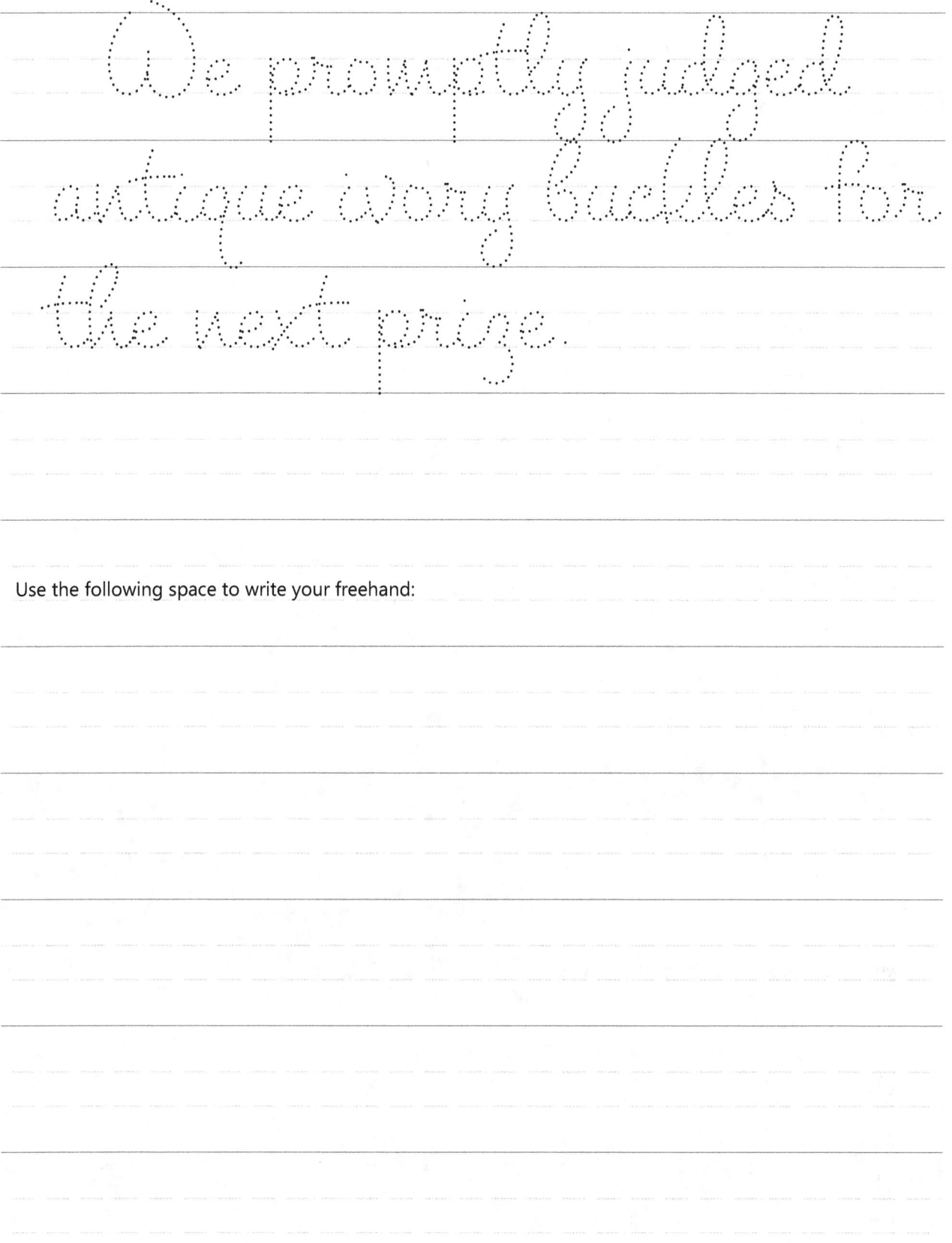

We promptly judged antique ivory buckles for the next prize.

Use the following space to write your freehand:

Saying:

Your success and happiness lie in you.

Trace the dotted words:

Your success and
happiness lie in you.
Your success and
happiness lie in you.

Handwriting Essential, trace the dotted letters:

& & & & & & &

? ? ? ? ? ? ?

Your success and

happiness lie in you.

Your success and

happiness lie in you.

Use the following space to write your freehand:

Pangram:

Pack my box with five dozen liquor jugs. (32 letters)

Trace the dotted words:

Pack my box with five

dozen liquor jugs.

Pack my box with five

dozen liquor jugs.

Handwriting Essential, trace the dotted letters:

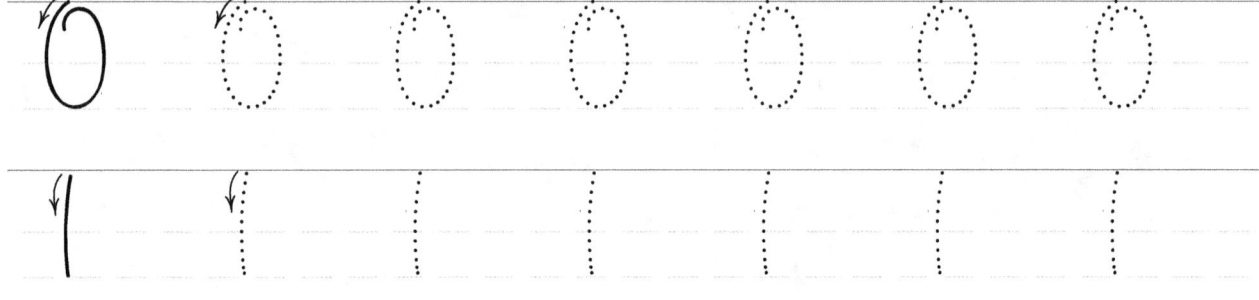

Pack my box with five dozen liquor jugs.

Pack my box with five dozen liquor jugs.

Use the following space to write your freehand:

Saying:

The best way to predict the future is to create it.

Trace the dotted words:

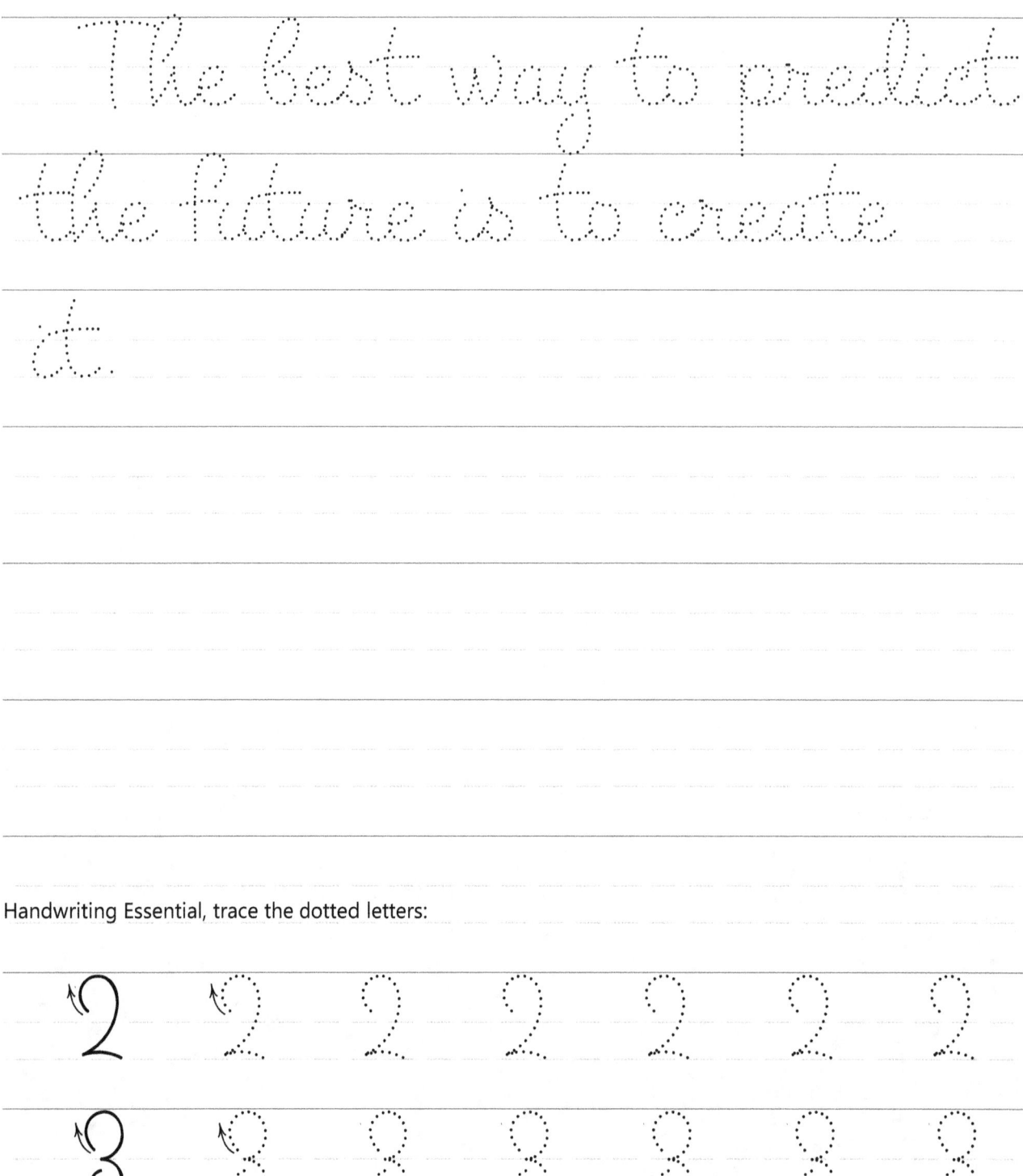

The best way to predict the future is to create it.

Handwriting Essential, trace the dotted letters:

2 2 2 2 2 2 2

3 3 3 3 3 3 3

The best way to predict the future is to create it.

Use the following space to write your freehand:

Pangram:

Jived fox nymph grabs quick waltz. (28 letters)

Trace the dotted words:

Jived fox nymph grabs

quick waltz.

Jived fox nymph grabs

quick waltz.

Handwriting Essential, trace the dotted letters:

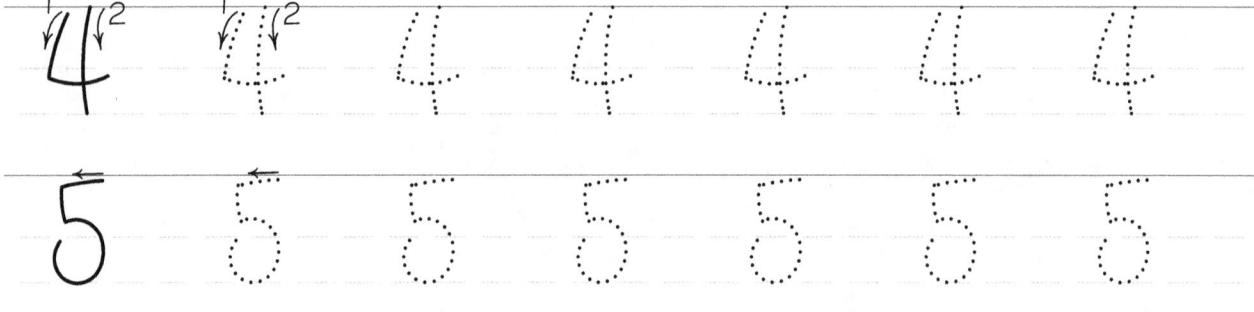

Jived fox nymph grabs quick waltz.

Jived fox nymph grabs quick waltz.

Use the following space to write your freehand:

Saying:

In a gentle way, you can shake the world.

Trace the dotted words:

In a gentle way, you can shake the world.

In a gentle way, you can shake the world.

Handwriting Essential, trace the dotted letters:

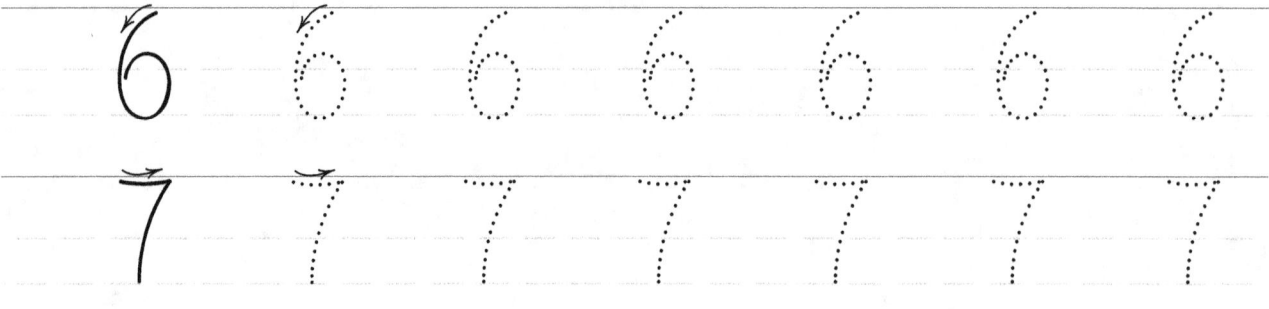

6 6 6 6 6 6 6

7 7 7 7 7 7 7

In a gentle way, you
can shake the world.

In a gentle way, you
can shake the world.

Use the following space to write your freehand:

Pangram:

Glib jocks quiz nymph to vex dwarf. (28 letters)

Trace the dotted words:

Glib jocks quiz nymph to vex dwarf.

Glib jocks quiz nymph to vex dwarf.

Handwriting Essential, trace the dotted letters:

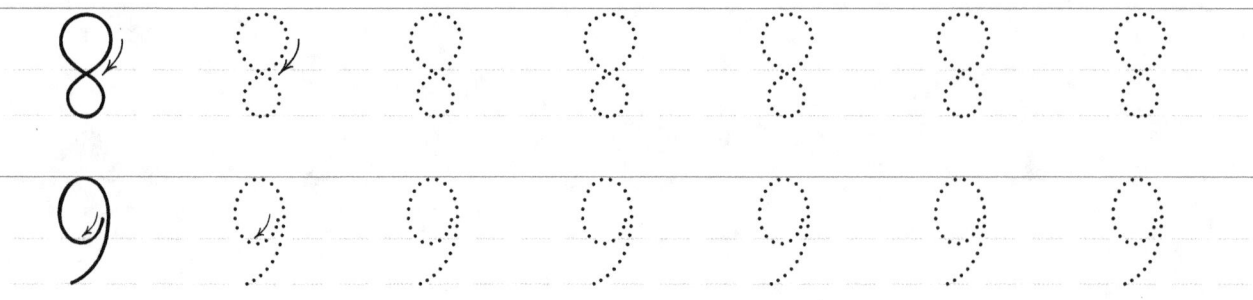

Glib jocks quiz nymph to vex dwarf.

Glib jocks quiz nymph to vex dwarf.

Use the following space to write your freehand:

Saying:

The way to get started is to quit talking and begin doing.

Trace the dotted words:

The way to get started
is to quit talking and
begin doing.

Handwriting Essential, trace the dotted letters:

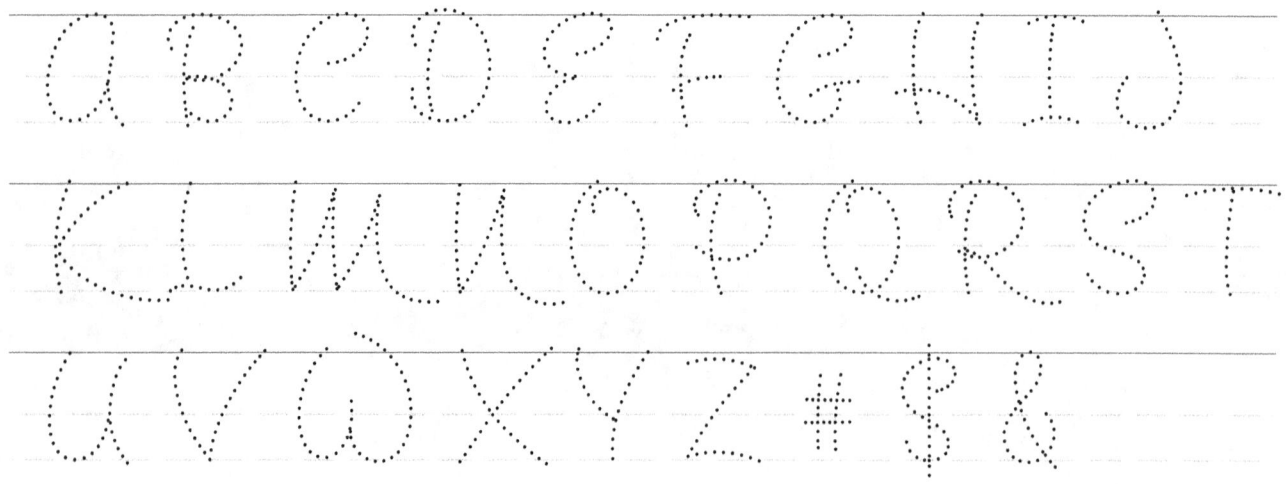

The way to get started is to quit talking and begin doing.

Use the following space to write your freehand:

Pangram:

Jackdaws love my big sphinx of quartz. (31 letters)

Trace the dotted words:

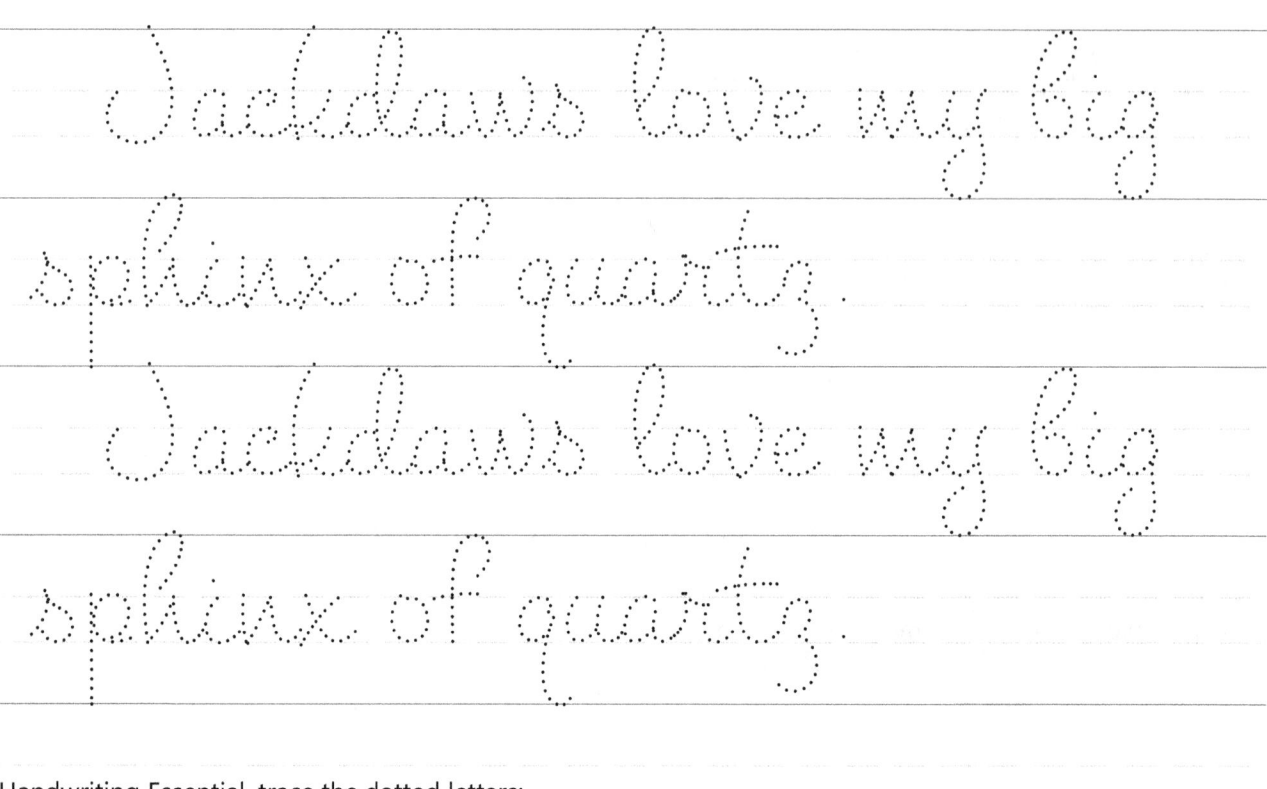

Jackdaws love my big

sphinx of quartz.

Jackdaws love my big

sphinx of quartz.

Handwriting Essential, trace the dotted letters:

a b c d e f g h i j k l m n

o p q r s t u v w x y z

1 2 3 4 5 6 7 8 9 0

Jackdaws love my big sphinx of quartz.

Jackdaws love my big sphinx of quartz.

Use the following space to write your freehand:

Saying:

It is the duty of the patriot to protect his country from its government.

Trace the dotted words:

It is the duty of the
patriot to protect his
country from its
government.

Handwriting Essential, trace the dotted letters:

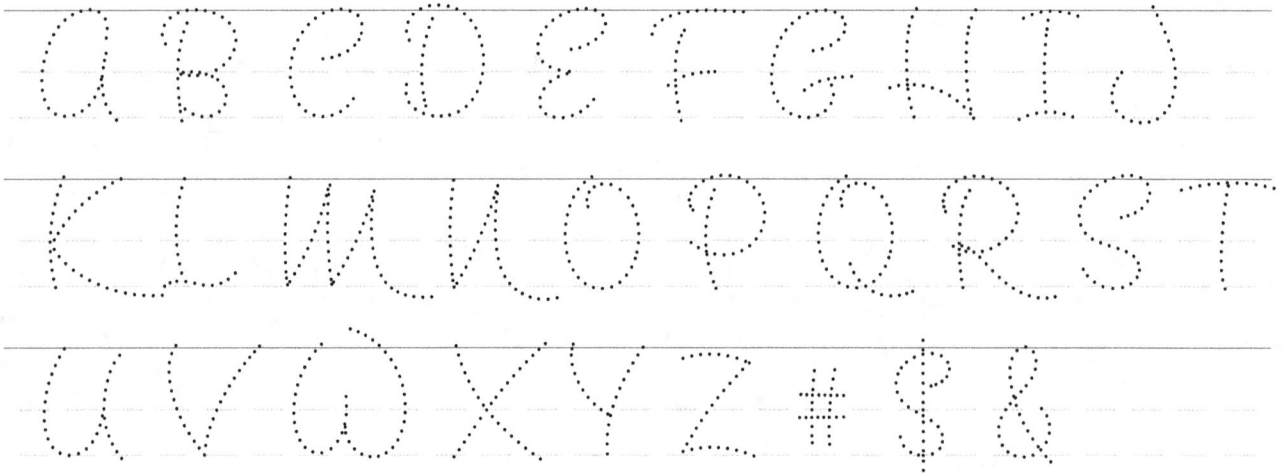

ABCDEFGHIJ
KLMNOPQRST
UVWXYZ # $ &

It is the duty of the patriot to protect his country from its government.

Use the following space to write your freehand:

Pangram:

The five boxing wizards jump quickly. (31 letters)

Trace the dotted words:

The five boxing

wizards jump quickly.

The five boxing

wizards jump quickly.

Handwriting Essential, trace the dotted letters:

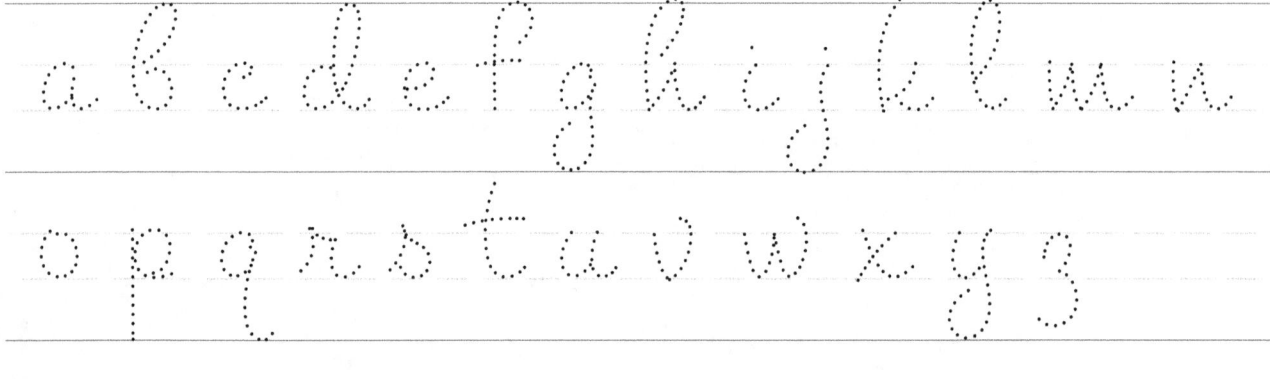

a b c d e f g h i j k l m n

o p q r s t u v w x y z

1 2 3 4 5 6 7 8 9 0

The five boxing

wizards jump quickly.

The five boxing

wizards jump quickly.

Use the following space to write your freehand:

Saying:

I didn't fall. The floor just needed a hug.

Trace the dotted words:

I didn't fall. The floor

just needed a hug.

I didn't fall. The floor

just needed a hug.

Handwriting Essential, trace the dotted letters:

A B C D E F G H I J

K L M N O P Q R S T

U V W X Y Z # $ &

I didn't fall. The floor

just needed a hug.

I didn't fall. The floor

just needed a hug.

Use the following space to write your freehand:

Pangram:

Zoo has animals called Bob, Party, Fog Junk, Wavy, and Quicxy. (44 letters)

Trace the dotted words:

Zoo has animals called
Bob, Party, Fog Junk,
Wavy, and Quicxy.

Handwriting Essential, trace the dotted letters:

a b c d e f g h i j k l m n

o p q r s t u v w x y z

1 2 3 4 5 6 7 8 9 0

Zoo has animals called
Bob, Party, Fog Dusk,
Davy, and Quiexy.

Use the following space to write your freehand:

Saying:

Honesty is the first chapter in the book of wisdom.

Trace the dotted words:

Honesty is the first
chapter in the book of
wisdom.

Handwriting Essential, trace the dotted letters:

A B C D E F G H I J
K L M N O P Q R S T
U V W X Y Z # $ &

Honesty is the first chapter in the book of wisdom.

Use the following space to write your freehand:

Pangram:

Zebra is just quite a very good implication of extra clear black and white. (61 letters)

Trace the dotted words:

Zebra is just quite a
very good implication of
extra clear black and
white.

Handwriting Essential, trace the dotted letters:

a b c d e f g h i j k l m n

o p q r s t u v w x y z

1 2 3 4 5 6 7 8 9 0

Zebra is just quite a very good implication of extra clear black and white.

Use the following space to write your freehand:

Saying:

To be old & wise, you must first have to be young & stupid.

Trace the dotted words:

To be old & wise, you
must first have to be
young & stupid.

Handwriting Essential, trace the dotted letters:

A B C D E F G H I J
K L M N O P Q R S T
U V W X Y Z # $ &

To be old & wise, you must first have to be young & stupid.

Use the following space to write your freehand:

Pangram:

Jocks fumbled the pizza quivering waxy. (33 letters)

Trace the dotted words:

Jocks fumbled the

pizza quivering waxy.

Jocks fumbled the

pizza quivering waxy.

Handwriting Essential, trace the dotted letters:

a b c d e f g h i j k l m n

o p q r s t u v w x y z

1 2 3 4 5 6 7 8 9 0

Jocks fumbled the

pizza quivering waxy.

Jocks fumbled the

pizza quivering waxy.

Use the following space to write your freehand:

Saying:

If you think nobody cares if you're alive, try missing a couple of car payments

Trace the dotted words:

If you think nobody cares if you're alive, try missing a couple of car payments

Handwriting Essential, trace the dotted letters:

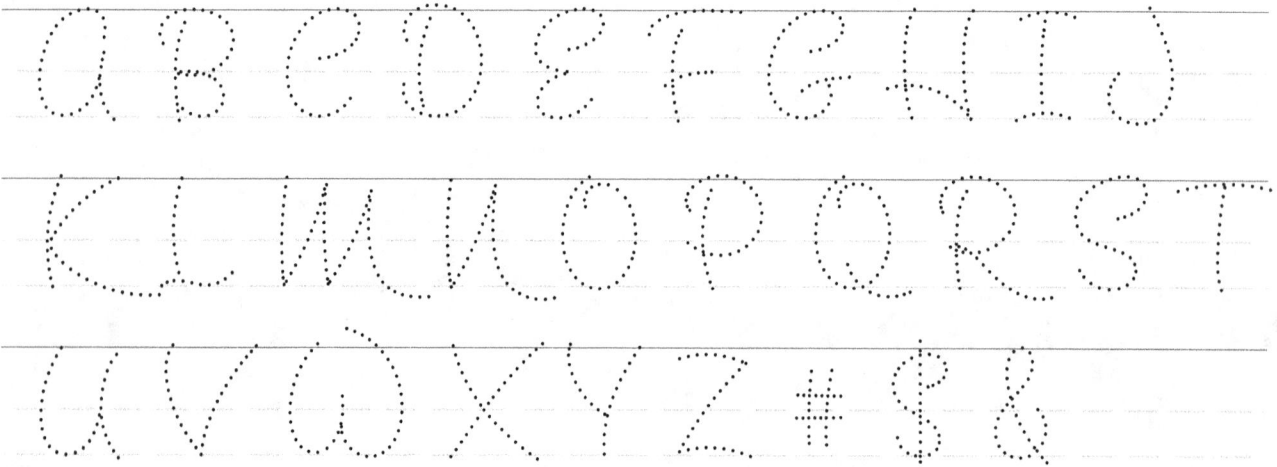

If you think nobody cares if you're alive, try missing a couple of car payments

Use the following space to write your freehand:

Pangram:

The jay, pig, fox, zebra, and my wolves quack! (33 letters)

Trace the dotted words:

The jay, pig, fox,
zebra, and my wolves
quack!

Handwriting Essential, trace the dotted letters:

a b c d e f g h i j k l m n

o p q r s t u v w x y z

1 2 3 4 5 6 7 8 9 0

The jay, pig, fox,
zebra, and my wolves
quack!

Use the following space to write your freehand:

Saying:

A computer once beat me at chess, but it was no match for me at the kicking box.

Trace the dotted words:

A computer once beat me at chess, but it was no match for me at the kicking box.

Handwriting Essential, trace the dotted letters:

A B C D E F G H I J

K L M N O P Q R S T

U V W X Y Z # $ &

A computer once beat me at chess, but it was no match for me at the kicking box.

Use the following space to write your freehand:

Pangram:

Sympathizing would fix Quaker objectives. (36 letters)

Trace the dotted words:

Sympathizing would

fix Quaker objectives.

Sympathizing would

fix Quaker objectives.

Handwriting Essential, trace the dotted letters:

a b c d e f g h i j k l m n

o p q r s t u v w x y z

1 2 3 4 5 6 7 8 9 0

Sympathizing would fix Quaker objectives.

Sympathizing would fix Quaker objectives.

Use the following space to write your freehand:

Saying:

You don't want a fifty-dollar haircut on a fifty-cent head.

Trace the dotted words:

You don't want a
fifty-dollar haircut on a
fifty-cent head.

Handwriting Essential, trace the dotted letters:

A B C D E F G H I J
K L M N O P Q R S T
U V W X Y Z # $ &

You don't want a
fifty-dollar haircut on a
fifty-cent head.

Use the following space to write your freehand:

Pangram:

A wizard's job is to vex chumps quickly in fog. (36 letters)

Trace the dotted words:

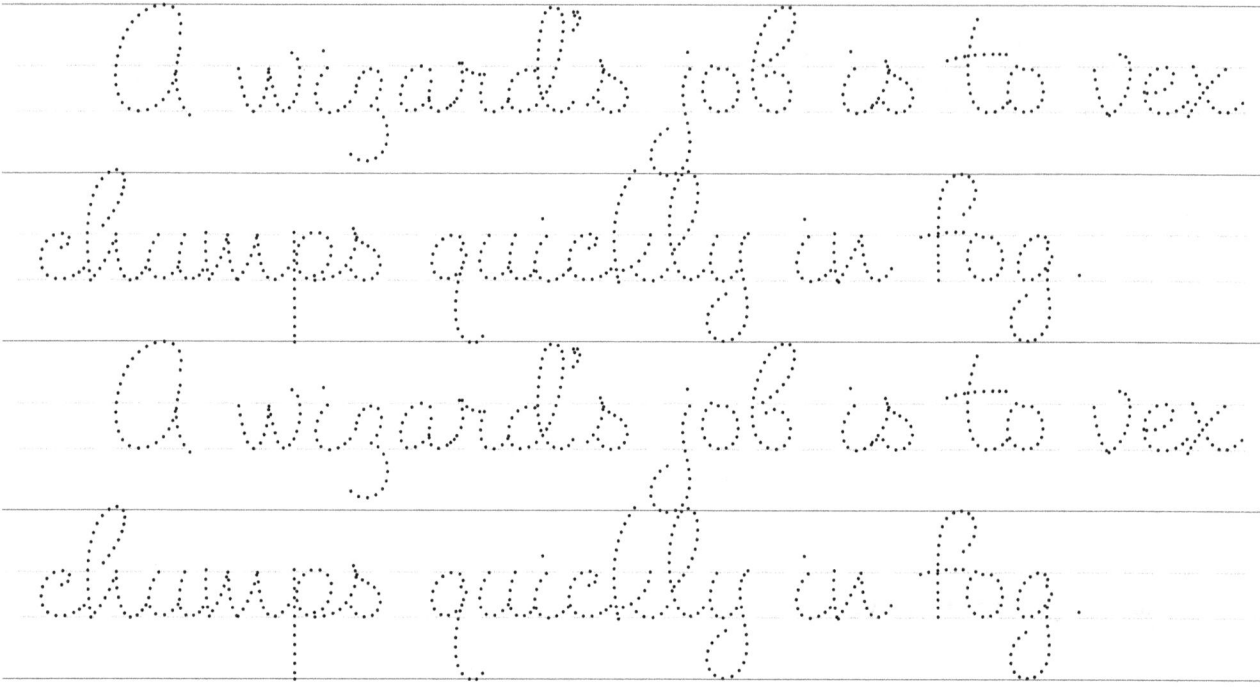

Handwriting Essential, trace the dotted letters:

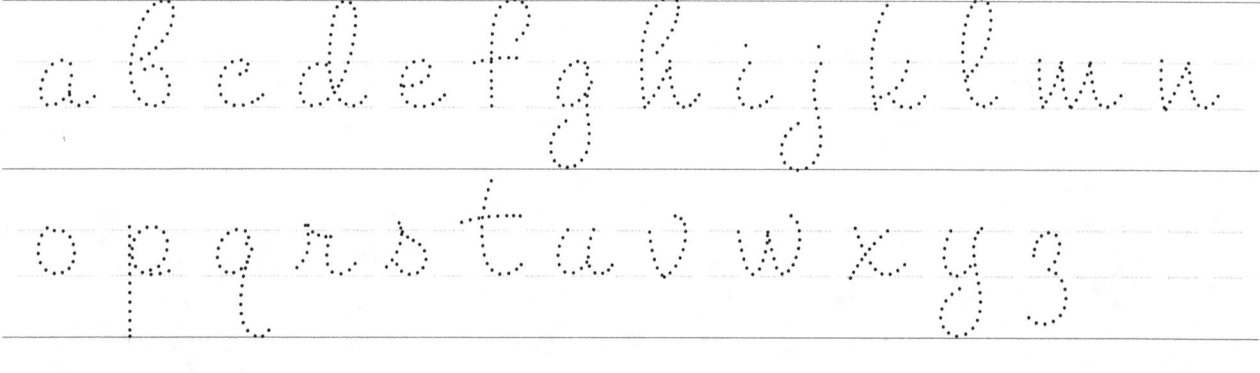

A wizard's job is to vex

chumps quickly in fog.

A wizard's job is to vex

chumps quickly in fog.

Use the following space to write your freehand:

Saying:

The hardest thing in the world to understand is income tax.

Trace the dotted words:

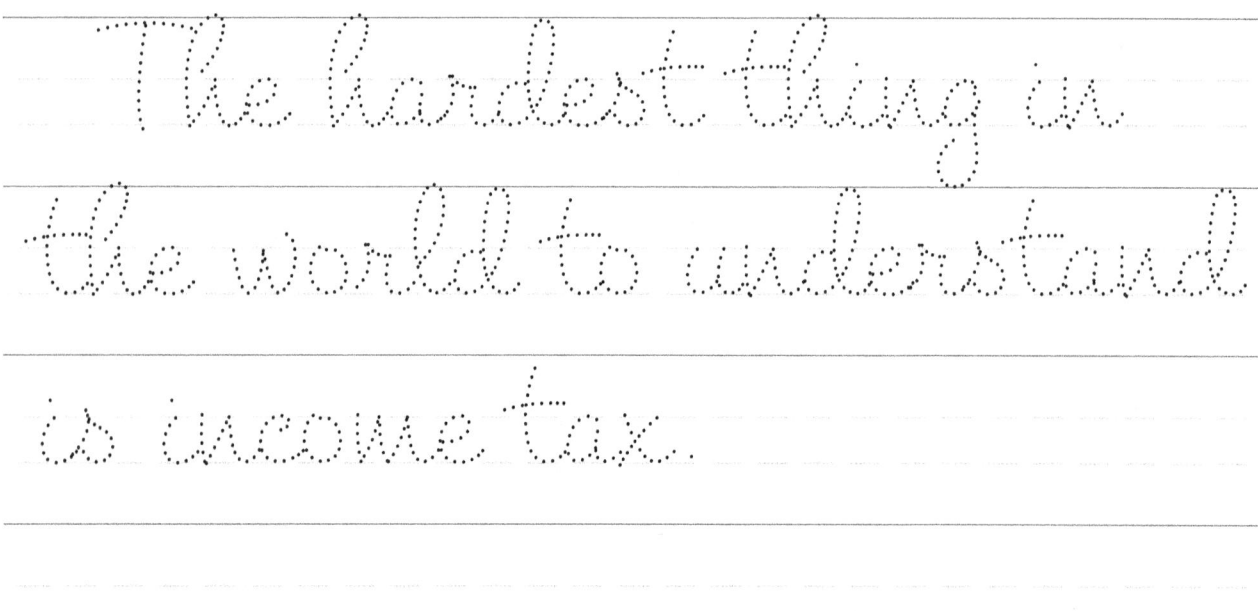

Handwriting Essential, trace the dotted letters:

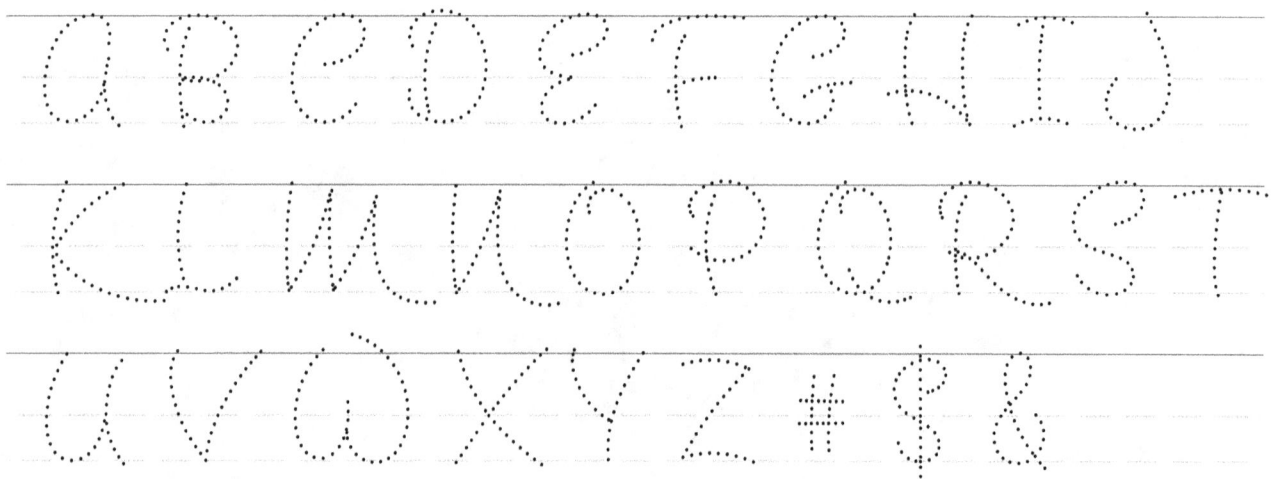

The hardest thing in
the world to understand
is income tax.

Use the following space to write your freehand:

Practice sheet

Epilogue

Congratulation! You have made thus far. I know your freehand writing is better than before you started to practice with this book. I genuinely hope so. That way, the whole thing would be worth the money you paid for this book or worth the book's value as the gift given to you. So what from now on? My suggestion is to start reading and practicing calligraphy with the foundation you have built with this book if you have time to do so. My favorite calligraphy books are Art of Calligraphy by David Harris (1995) and Writing, Illuminating & Lettering by Edward Johnston (1906). The books are for right-handed. But art has no left or right, thinking about famous lefties like Leonardo da Vinci or Michelangelo Buonarroti. Besides, it more fun breaking the right-sided bias when learning and practicing calligraphy with these right-handed books.

Calligraphy is a visual art. You might not be able to monetize it directly. Consider the creative mindset cultivated by art training; it's the creativity that subconsciously influences your behavior, lifestyle, and work habits. It's the creativities and aesthetic taste stimulated by the sense of art that does the tricks. See the graceful designs of Apple products, Macs, iPhones, and iPads. Tech icon Steve Jobs recalled at his famous 2005 commencement address at Stanford University that Palladino's calligraphy class he took at Reed College inspired ultimately the elegance for which Apple computers are renowned. He had three courses at Reed College before dropping out of college. Calligraphy, Dance, and Shakespea.

Calligraphing is a process of creation. An essential value of calligraphy, sometimes lettering, for me, is meditation. The creation process easily alters my focus and calms me down quickly. I can write the word F$$K over hundreds of different ways, and I don't need to tell who they're for when I sketch the angry F&$Ks. It's fun. It's better than drawing an ugly face on a golf ball before taking it to a course and hitting it away. It's too much work to draw and isn't worth the time.

Again, thank you for practicing handwriting with this book. You have made at least one of my works useful. It means so much to me, and thank you!

Thank you!

from the most delicate parts of my heart!

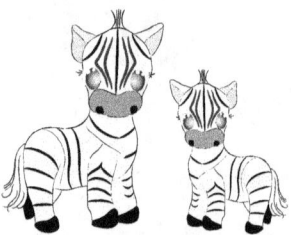